DEDICATION

The Keys to Life Holy Bible prayed is dedicated to those I love who labor in the ministry of the Gospel of Jesus Christ. A special thanks to my family, my wife Sieglinda my helper from God to complete me and the love of my life. I could not have written this prayer book with out you.

If you pray it he will come

Andrew, Servant of God the Father and the Lord Jesus Christ

The Keys to Life ©

Scripture turned Prayer Book

Praying God's Word back to Him

What is Prayer?

Prayer is the connection between your soul (mind) and the soul (mind) of God, not in concentration or meditation, but in direct communication with Him.

It is earnestly seeking the Lord, pouring out the soul before the Lord, praying and crying to heaven, seeking God and making supplication. It is drawing near to God.

I believe prayer should be personal and intimate, but **out loud**.

The Bible is a Book of Prayers

The Bible teaches that all the Disciples, all the Apostles, and all true Believers pray without ceasing. The Bible is our source of literally thousands of prayers when we pray the Word of the Lord back to the Lord. In this book, I've written prayers for various occasions in our lives that, hopefully, will serve as a guide to help you in your prayer life. In everything, we are to give thanks, for this is the will of God concerning us. We are encouraged to let the Spirit flow freely in our prayers.

What Happens When You Pray?

You build *relationships* with God. Pray so we all may be one, as the Father, and Jesus are one. Pray that you also may be one in Them. Pray that the world will believe that God sent Jesus to live in all who seek the all-righteous unseen heavenly Father.
Pray for Authority over your flesh.

God says He will give us the keys to the kingdom of heaven. One of those keys is the authority over the evil one who comes to disrupt our lives and the authority to pray for God's fruits of the Spirit or the gifts of the Spirit when we need them and for His blessings. Whatever we bind (pray) on Earth, it is bound (prayed) in heaven: and whatever we loose on Earth, it is loosed in heaven.
Jesus instructs His followers to Pray without ceasing

He said for our sakes that He sanctified Himself so we would be sanctified through the truth. He didn't just pray for His disciples and followers who were with Him at the time of His crucifixion, He prayed for all of us who might believe in Him based on the word of the disciples and apostles - you and me who believe based on the Word of God that has been taught through the ages. Using Jesus as a model for praying, Scriptures tell us that He fell on his face and prayed. He prayed two, three or four times in one night. He withdrew to the wilderness from all distractions and prayed. He prayed so hard that His appearance was altered.

My Inspiration

"But there is a spirit in man: and the inspiration of the Almighty gives us understanding." - Job 32:8 KJV

I was sitting in Bible study conducted by my pastor at the time, Terry L. Harris, of Tacoma Christian Center in Tacoma, Washington. He began to share some Scriptures that he said helped him in his Christian walk over the past 15 years.

I thought that I would bless my pastor by taking the Scriptures out of Ephesians Chapter One and turn them into a prayer. As I began to read the Scriptures in the form of a prayer, the Lord began to lead me into making the entire chapter into a personal prayer - you know, praying for yourself. It's me, O Lord, who is standing in the need of prayer.

As I began to change other Scriptures into personal prayers, I became driven to the task. Then the Lord placed in my Spirit that I was going to write 66 Bible-based prayers.

The anointing became so wonderful and great that I would spend seven or more hours a day changing scripture into prayers and then praying them back to the Lord.

One of the many blessings I now enjoy is a very intimate relationship with the Lord and I enjoy hearing and recognizing God's voice all day long. I guess you could say that I am now what God's Word describes as a "peculiar person." All I want to do is pray, talk with the God, and read the Bible.

Some of the prayers are long, some are not so long. The reason for this is, as I searched the Bible for scriptures to write the prayers, the Holy Spirit would show me which ones to use in the prayer.

Why Long Prayers?

What is the advantage and blessings in praying for long periods of time?

Let's use Jesus praying in the Garden of Gethsemane before He was crucified as an example of praying for long periods of time. He prayed for such a long time that when He returned the first time, He found His disciples sleeping.

He told them to watch and pray so that they would not fall into temptation. He noted that the spirit may have been willing, but the body was weak.

Jesus was in a battle between the natural man and the spiritual man, between flesh and Spirit. By this time, Jesus had begun to take on the full nature of man. He said during that prayer time that His "soul is overwhelmed with sorrow to the point of death." I believe that those words did not come from the Spirit man in Jesus; they came from the flesh man.

When you pray, God is there, and yes, the Devil is there also, or at least he is represented. You are trying to be spiritual, but Satan's ambassadors are trying to prevent you from being spiritual. That's their job, to make you to rely on your flesh. But God also sends His angels to comfort you during that time and minister to your Spirit.

Jesus was in a battle trying to stay focused on His mission and accomplish it. It was a long spiritual fight to stay focused and hear God's voice. Jesus had to continually to remind Himself why He was sent and that He was the only one who could make the atonement, not my will, but Your will be don Father.

By the same token, we are in a war where the forces of darkness are trying to capture our souls and make us live by the flesh and not the Spirit.

We will feel sleepy or distractions will come when we try to pray for long periods of time, but we must persevere and depend on the Lord for strength in our time of need.

The Word of God tells us in Ephesians that we are not fighting against people made of flesh and blood, but against the evil rulers and authorities of the unseen world, against those mighty powers of darkness who rule this world, and against wicked spirits in the heavenly realms. Use every piece of God's armor to resist the enemy in the time of evil, so that after the battle you will still be standing firm.

There are situations that require fasting and fervent praying. Satan's forces will resist you and see how strong you are and how strong your faith is. To me, I don't believe you can do that with short prayers.

Jesus is saying if you can't even endure a little struggle while you are trying to stay focused when you are praying, how will you do when the temptations from the forces of evil harass you, therefore making the assignment much harder for you to stay focused?

The Old Testament Prophet Daniel prayed for three weeks before a messenger from God arrived to give him an answer to his prayer. He was persistent and faithful in his prayer and didn't know there were forces fighting against him to keep the angel from getting to Him. But our God and his forces prevailed. God sent the war angel to fight off the evil so the messenger angel could get through to Daniel.

I pray that when that time comes you will be enabled to pray for long periods of time.

I remember when I would fight to pray for more than ten minutes.

I don't know about you, but I had a very hard time trying to stay focused when I prayed for any length of time. I would lose track of what I was praying. My mind would drift and I would have a difficult time staying awake, sometimes worse than other times. When the Bible talks about vain repetitions, it is talking about me.

I don't know about you, but I do not have the vocabulary or the memory that will allow me the words to express the blessings and benefits that comes with praying.

Prayers and Scriptures one in the same

For those Christians among us who just don't have the time to both read the Bible and pray regularly, The Keys to Life Prayer Book, may be just the right gift.

You can have both with The Keys to Life Prayer Book. You can pray and read the Bible at the same time because they are one in the same. Experience the power.

Why Pray Out Loud and Why Pray Scripture?

When God created the heavens and the Earth, He spoke things into existence. That tells me that God enjoyed hearing His own voice, how much more would your voice please Him?

When God speaks, His Word goes out and accomplishes what it says. When He said *out loud*, "Let there be light," there was light. When God said *out loud*, "Let the water under the sky be gathered into one place, and let the dry land appear." And it was so. When God said *out loud*, "Let Us make man in our image, according to our likeness, it was done.

Here are some benefits of praying out loud:
First

You hear yourself praying. You hear your prayers, which build your faith that comes, by hearing the Words of God. Your Spirit man hears you pray. God's word is food to your Spirit and this further builds your faith in God. Remember: You are the only one who can make sure your Spirit man gets fed.

When you pray out loud, amazing things begin to happen to you.

When you pray out loud, God ministers to you.

When you pray out loud, God's Word stretches you.

When you pray out loud, God's Word convicts you.

When you pray out loud, God's Word grows in you.

When you pray out loud to God, it makes Him talk to you.

Second

The angels that God has assigned to you hear you speaking, praying God's Word. I don't know if you know this or not, but angels only react to God's Word. Moreover, they can't read your mind. They must hear you. So pray out loud.

Third

When you pray out loud, the demons and fallen angels Satan has assigned to you also hear you praying God's Word. Demons react to God's Word and tremble. However, they can't read your mind. They must hear you. Pray out loud.

Fourth

When you pray out loud, God hears you. When you pray God's own Words back to God, you are reminding God of His own Word, and His own promises. God likes that.

When you pray the Bible, you will have no problem with watching and praying with Jesus for hours.

I don't know about you, but I have tried to pray Scriptures, straight from the Bible. One problem I encountered was that I had to concentrate on not only trying to make my reading the Bible sound and feel like a prayer, but I had to substitute one word for another.

Example: When God is talking to a nation, I would have to remember to change the word nation to me, my, I, or something like that. When God says I, I had to figure out if God meant Him or me - all this while still trying to pray. That won't be a problem when you pray the Key's to Life.

Anointed Scriptures

The Scripture-based prayers that the Lord has commissioned me to write are nothing more than already anointed Scriptures turned into personal prayers.

One Christian man asked me, why should I read your prayers? This is a man who does not pray much anyway. I had already pondered the question in my mind, weighed it, deliberated, soberly and deeply - why did God put the need to write the prayers in my Spirit?

After much prayer and asking the Lord Why me? I believe God said, "Just as He used real people to write the Bible, He uses real people to write books to support the Bible today. It's the same anointing of the same Holy Spirit."

So I responded that "first of all, they are not my prayers, they are the Word of God made into a personal prayer for you to pray back to God." Experience the benefits that come from the inspired Word of God, prayed back to God, out loud.

All of the prayers contained in The Keys to Life prayer Book are God's Word and are written under the Inspiration of The Holy Ghost. Test the Spirit!

When God's anointing would come over me to write, I would sit for hours changing God's Word into personal prayers.

My wife once said: "Baby, it's good that you are doing such a work for the Lord but you have others things to do also." But writing Bible based Scriptural Prayers was all I wanted to do and all I could do for the season. After a short period of rest from turning Bible Scripture into prayer, I am back at it again, and I'm loving it.

As a family, we come together three or four times a week and pray some of the prayers together. On the weekend we have family devotion as we learn the meaning of the prayers we pray, because they are the Word of God. This truly blesses us as a family. We also individually pray from The Keys to Life Prayer Book.

When I am going through something I pray the prayer that is appropriate for the moment. Right away my assigned angels begin to minister to me, because I am praying God's Word and I am lifted up.

THE POWER IN PRAYING GOD'S WORD

There is so much power in praying the prayers in "The Key's to Life", Because first, they are the anointed word of God, by praying these Anointed prayers, what you are doing is, using God's own system. In short, you are tapping into the heart of God's working power with a lasting revelations, and new understandings. How can a child get an understanding of what his/her parent wants if the parent never talks to them? While praying The Keys to Life Prayers, not only are you talking to Daddy God, but you are also talking God's language.

And as a double bonus, you hear The LORD talk to you, giving you a better understanding of His Holy Word. One that is lasting and life changing.

Have you ever been invited by someone to get involved in multilevel marketing? I have tried many and all with the same outcome. I never even got back my initial investment, unless I took advantage of a friend.

I soon learned to ask this one question: "How much money have you made?" They would always say the same thing, "well I haven't made anything yet, but so and so has." Then I would say, "come see me when you have."

What I am telling you is this fact, straight from the horse's mouth. The prayers in the "Keys to Life" Prayer book are tested and I Andrew Parker, a servant of God the Father and The Lord Jesus Christ, am walking in the fruits.

The prayers are proven to give "Life." It's as if God Himself has given us His own Bible Handbook that is designed to help us understand just how important reading the Bible is by bringing us into this understanding through praying His Word back to Him, *out loud*.

Because the Holy Spirit is the author. (And I am only the vessel used to write). This is what the Lord said. "The Keys to Life Prayer Book will be where ever the Bible is, in every language and in every style.

My wife and I pray all the prayers in the book on a regular basis. Our entire relationship is complete with Jesus as the center. And we don't need Viagra.

I wish I could tell you all the blessings praying "The Keys to Life" prays has done for us. But I will try; these are some of the blessings my wife, family and I now enjoy.

Praying the prayers on a regular basis has given us divine guidance; I could use many examples, but the best example I can use is my marriage.

Now our entire marriage is truly made in Heaven, we enjoy each other better than in any other time in our entire relationship of more than 30 years because we now truly understand each of our rolls in the marriage.

Praying the prayers on a regular basis has led us to truly understand the concept of creation, when God brought Eve to Adam. How He established the institution of marriage and family.

The human rights to each family member as well and most importantly, the rights to our Spiritual inheritance, and how they affect the entire family structure.

Praying the prayers on a regular basis has led us into understanding that everything we do for our natural person we must make sure we do the Very same thing for our Spiritual person.

Praying the prayers on a regular basis has led us into a place where we do not allow our natural person to make choices that are our Spiritual person's right to make.

Praying the prayers on a regular basis has led us into a better understanding of the Bible that makes reading the Bible fun, and has changed us into people who want to make an earnest effort to obey what it says.

Praying the prayers on a regular basis has led us into a more personal and intimate relationship with Jesus Christ, the Holy Spirit and even God the Father Himself.

Praying the prayers on a regular basis has led us into a place where our mind and heart has really opened up to joyfully receive the things of God. Praying the prayers on a regular basis has brought about true conviction that has lead to true repentance in all areas in our life. Praying the prayers on a regular basis has led us to genuinely feel good about our feelings concerning this new relationship we are now into with God.

Praying the prayers on a regular basis has led us into thirsting more and more for Gods wisdom, understanding and love.

Praying the prayers on a regular basis has led us into a safe place with God. Praying the prayers on a regular basis has led us into wanting to be the man and woman God wants us to be. The funny part about this is we want to become just that. Praying the prayers on a regular basis has led us into greater faith because we are discovering that God is everything He says He is. In short, praying the prayers on a regular basis has led us into a place to where we do what we pray.

Prayer Book, the voice of The Lord came and we had one-on-one fellowship for seven days. The Lord came on Monday, August 15, 2005, and left on August 21, 2005, three days later He came back. I asked Him:

"Why did you leave?" (I thought that I had done something wrong that made him leave). The LORD said, "First, you see me, then you don't see me, then you see me." Then He left, but He left me with this feeling, I would be visited by Him again not only in the life to come, but in this same way in this life.

Seven days later the Holy Spirit Came all over me in a way so different that I felt as though I was pretending to have a relationship before this. Now I know I have relationships with Jesus Christ, the Holy Spirit and even God the Father all day long. Because I continue to pray and study The Holy Bible, the Heavenly Father continues to take deeper and deeper into His love

My Prayer for You

Father, in Jesus' name, I pray that You will send a special double dose of Your Anointing to everyone who prays the prayers in this book with these facts in mind:

THE KEY TO PRAYING IS HEARING.

THE KEY TO PRAYING GOD'S OWN WORDS BACK TO HIM IS THAT IT UNLOCKS HEAVEN FOR YOU TO HEAR THE VOICE OF THE LORD RIGHT HERE ON EARTH.

Andrew, a servant of God the Father and the Lord Jesus Christ

TABLE OF CONTENTS

Introduction..01

A time for everything..22

After Gods own heart..24

For a Caleb Spirit...26

For a mighty prince of valor...................................28

For a new heart..31

For achievement-prosperity-success......................33

For an open mind..35

For anxiety..37

For approaching death..39

For authority to loose God's blessings...................41

For being a mighty man of valor............................43

For being a parent..46

For being a virtuous princess..................................48

For being a virtuous woman...................................51

For cheerfulness..54

For Christ to dwell in my heart...............................56

For comfort...57

For convalescence...58

For endurance..60

For fairness..63

For faith..64

For forgiveness..66

For faithfulness...68

For frankness..70

For gaining wealth...72

For God's full blessing......................................74

For God's wisdom..75

For gratitude..78

For happiness...80

Our family prayer..82

For honoring parents.......................................84

For hope...86

For humility...88

For keeping me today.......................................91

Let go and let God...93

For lifting up my family before God......................94

For authority in loosing and binding.....................97

For making correct decisions..............................99

The Lord is my Shepherd..................................101

For married couples..102

For married man..104

For married women..107

For disappointments..110

For nightly protection...112

For God's Power..115

For power to not gossip.....................................118

For repentance..120

For the revelation of Jesus Christ.....................122

Forsake me not O Lord......................................123

For salvation..124

For seeking God First...126

For self-control..128

For spiritual eyes...130

For spiritual warfare..132

For the Lord is my shepherd II..........................135

For the ability to love..140

For the baptism of the Holy Spirit.....................143

For the fruits of the Spirit...................................145

For the Lord's Prayer..149

Magnificent is the name of the Lord................152

For the power to pray...153

For trusting in God..156

For truthfulness……………………………………..158

For unselfishness……………………………………160

For when I am weak He is strong…………………162

For when I fall down……………………………….164

For believing God……………………………………166

For praying God's Word………………………………..167

For putting on the whole armor of God………………..171

Authors Note ……………………………………….173

Credits Acknowledgements………………………..174

Appendix……………………………………………..175

A TIME FOR ALL THINGS

Father, in Heaven let Your name be honored, let Your kingdom come, let Your will be done here on earth just as it is in heaven.

Father, as You give me my food for today, it is my prayer, that You will open my eyes, so wide that I will clearly see the times in which my life is facing right now; a time that is testing my faith. Father, help me to stand not in my faith only, but in Your ever increasing faith.

Father, Your Word teaches that there will be a time and a season for everything.

A time and a season for every activity under Heaven. A time to be born and a time to die. A time to plant and a time to harvest. A time to kill and a time to heal. A time to tear down and a time to rebuild. A time to cry and a time to laugh. A time to grieve and a time to dance. A time to scatter stones and a time to gather stones.

A time to embrace and a time to turn away. A time to search and a time to lose. A time to keep and a time to throw away. A time to tear and a time to mend. A time to be quiet and a time to speak up.

A time to love and a time to hate. A time for war and a time for peace.

Lord I pray that You will show me how to live the abundant life at all times. Father, Jesus said "the thief comes to steal, to kill and to destroy: But that You sent Him to give life and to give it more abundantly in all times."

Father, Jesus also said, "I assure You, that everyone who has in various times given up house or wife or brothers or parents or children, for the sake of the Kingdom of God, will be repaid many times over in this life, as well as receiving eternal life in the world to come."

Father, You made everything beautiful for its own time. You planted eternity in my heart, but even so I cannot see the whole scope of Your work from beginning to end.

Lord I have concluded that there is nothing better for me than to be happy and to enjoy myself at all times for as long as I can. That I should eat, drink, and enjoy the fruits of my labor, for these are gifts from You.

Father, help me to know what time I am in and how to live right when I am in that time. Father, Your word says it is getting late; time is running out.

In Jesus' Name I pray, Amen

AFTER GOD'S OWN HEART

Father, You gave this testimony: "I have found David, the son of Jesse, a man after My own heart, who shall fulfill all My will."

Father, Your Word teaches this does not imply that David was perfect but that he sought to do Your will. Instead of showing stubborn disobedience, he exhibited nobility of purpose and sought the welfare of the people, and aimed at living a pure life.

Father, I pray that just like David, You will help me to seek Your will and even if I fall seven times, You will raise me up again. Father, I pray, help me to understand it is not enough to just get back up again, but to get back in the race.

Lord make me wise in heart and mind, and mighty in Your strength, so that if I sin against anyone and in Your sight, I will be like David, and repent right away and become wiser than before. Father, help me love You in the same manor that You love me.

Father, help me to realize that You love me so much, that Your mercy endure and is every lasting. Father, I pray that like David, when I fall let me fall into Your hands, for Your mercies are great.

Father, help me to be confident of the very fact, that You have begun a good work in me and will perform it until the day Jesus Christ comes for me.

Lord I confess to You all my sins and I pray have mercy on me and forgive me.

Father, show me how to make You proud of me, and when I ask for Your forgiveness, take me back. Father, put me back in the race. I love You! I pray that You will teach me how to walk upright. Father, help me to break every bad habit and loose me from every addiction.

Lord Jesus, come into my heart, live in me and teach me. Father, I give my whole self to You. Please, heal me, Lord. You are my God, and I am Your child.

In Jesus' Name I pray,

Amen

FOR A CALEB SPIRIT

Lord I pray for You to develop in me a different Spirit, one with the likeness of the Spirit Caleb possessed, so when You speak to me I will recognize Your voice. Lord I pray that You give me a different Spirit, one in the likeness of the Spirit Joshua possessed, and I will follow You fully.

Thank You Heavenly Father, for revealing to me the height, length, breadth and depths of Your love. Lord I pray that You will bring me into a rich land flowing with milk and honey, so my family and I will possess it.

Lord I pray in my Lord and Savior Jesus Christ's name, not only for a bold, generous, courageous, noble and heroic Spirit; but a Spirit that is totally capable of raising me up above human emotions and earthly fears. Therefore, I will submit to You fully, for You are my maker.

Lord as I continue to pray Your Word into my Spirit, I will continue to walk in the Holy Spirit and live in the Holy Spirit. Father, I promise to encourage all people everywhere I go, to go right away and take the land that You promised us. "For we certainly will conquer it!" Father, with a different Spirit, I will know that we can take every giant in the land.

Lord I also pray that You will bring me and my loved ones safely into the land of promise, and give it to us. Lord I pray that I will not rebel against You and that I will not be afraid of the people of the land. For they are helpless prey to me because You are always with me.

I Give You unlimited Praise Lord for You have shown me that Your Power is as great as You have claimed it to be. Lord I thank You for being patient with me. You have proven to be slow to anger and rich in unfailing love concerning me. You have forgiven every kind of sin and rebellion.

Lord like such believers as Joshua and Caleb, I take You at Your Word. I realize that no weapons that the enemy may form against me can prosper. I know that as long as I walk in Your might and Your strength, I will prevail. Father, I pledge to follow You fully, so I will receive the height, length, breadth, and depth of Your Eternal Love and Salvation.

Lord I praise You, for now I am standing fast in liberty because Christ has made me free and I am no longer entangled in the yoke of bondage.

In Jesus' Name I pray,

Amen

MIGHTY PRINCE OF VALOR

Father, I have fixed my thoughts on what is true, honorable, and right. Holy Spirit, thank You for making me think about things that are pure and lovely and admirable. Lord Jesus, it's because of You that I think about things that are excellent and worthy of praise.

Thank You, Holy Spirit, for making me keep putting into practice all that I have learned and heard from the Father, and now the Lord's peace is with me. How grateful I am, and how I praise You, Lord because You are concerned about me. Father, I know You have always been and always will be concerned about me.

Father, for a time I didn't know just how much You could help me, not that I thought I was not in need of Your help. Lord I pray for You to teach me how to be happy whether I have much or less.

Holy Spirit, teach me the secret of living in every situation, whether it is with a full stomach or an empty stomach, with plenty or less. Father, I know that I can do everything with the help of Christ, because through Him, You have given me the strength I need.

Father, because of Your grace, I have victory in everything that I do. I give You thanks for making my life a successful one. Lord You sent Your messenger Angel, and He continues to remind me, that You are always with me, because I am a Mighty Prince of Valor.

O Lord I thank You, because You are with me, I cannot fail because You have made me a Mighty Prince of Valor. And my enemies cannot stand against the strength and courage You have given me, because I am a Mighty Prince of Valor.

I give You praises, Father for I am a Mighty Prince of Valor when it comes to my health, and my wealth. I am a Mighty Prince of Valor when it comes to my faith and power. I am a Mighty Prince of Valor when it comes to being a Valiant Prince. Father, I am a Mighty Prince of Valor when I am at war with my flesh, because You are always there to give me the victory over my flesh.

Father, You have made me the ruler over all things in the whole Earth. Father, You have made me an honorable Mighty Prince of Valor, because You have made my heart Your Home. Father, help me to dedicate my life to only You always.

Father, because Your goodness endured continually in me, I am a Mighty Prince of Valor. I praise You, Lord for You have made me a wise Mighty Prince of Valor, with confidence, so as I judge all things,

I will be prudent. Father, as a Mighty Prince of Valor, I pray that You will always keep me humble.

Father, I pledge that as a Mighty Prince of Valor, my glory will rests in Your Wisdom, and I know that the works I do will not be done in vain. Father, In Your Wisdom I will do mighty works.

Father, I Praise You because You have given me the victory, with authority in Your power to do all things, for all that is in the heaven and in the Earth belongs to You. For Yours is the kingdom of God. O Lord my God, You are exalted as head above all.

Father, thank You for calling me Your son. And now all people will know that I am a Mighty Prince of Valor.

In Jesus' Name I pray,

Amen

FOR A NEW HEART

Father, I pray that You will give me a new heart, so You can put a new Spirit in me as You take the stony heart out of my flesh and give me a new heart for my flesh.

Father, I claim Your Word where You said to me that You would give me a new heart, a whole new system of renewed affections. And that You will put a new Spirit within me to direct and influence these new affections.

Father, I pray that You take the stony heart out of my flesh, the one that cannot receive the impressions of Your Spirit and replace it with a heart that can receive the impressions of Your Spirit. One that is capable of receiving and retaining these impressions.

Father, I thank You for revealing to me through Your Word, that no man can put new wine into old skins, else the new wine will burst the skins and spill and the skins shall perish. But new wine must be put into new skins and both are preserved.

Father, in the same manner, no man can put new impressions of Your Spirit into a stony heart, because a stony heart is not capable of receiving Spiritual impressions. Lord I pray take the stony heart from me and replace it with a new heart that I can forgive others as You forgive me.

Father, I pray that I will be committed and remain committed in my belief that the Bible is true and I pray that when I begin to deal with specific Bible passages, I will always defend the truth of the Bible and I will not back away.

In Jesus' Name I pray,

Amen

FOR ACHIEVEMENT, PROSPERITY, AND SUCCESS

O Lord what joy I experience when I do not follow the advice of the wicked, or stand around with sinners, or join in with mockers.

For my delight is in doing everything my Lord wants, both day and night.

I am like a tree planted along the riverbank, bearing fruit each season without fail. And my leaves never wither, and in all I do, I prosper.

Father, Help me to never forget the things You have taught me. Father, help me to always store Your commands in my heart, for they will give me a long and satisfying life.

Father, help me to never let my loyalty and kindness to You and others, get away from me. Father, help me to wear loyalty and kindness like a necklace, and to write them deep within my heart. Then I will find favor with both You, and others, and I will gain a good reputation.

Father, I pray, help me to always trust in You, with all my heart, and to not depend on my own understanding. Father, I pray, help me to always seek Your will in all I do, and to trust You to direct my paths.

Father, I pray, help me to always commit all my work to You, so that all my plans will succeed.

Father, help me listen to Your instruction so I will prosper; Father, Your Word says "those who trust in You, will be happy." "And that good planning and hard work lead to prosperity, but hasty shortcuts lead to poverty." But, true humility and fear of You, lead to riches, honor, and long life.

People who cover over their sins will not prosper. But when I confess and forsake my sins, I will receive mercy, because trusting You, leads to heavenly prosperity. Father, I pray, help me to be sharpened in Your Wisdom, because the value of Your Wisdom will help me to succeed.

In Jesus' Name I pray,

Amen

FOR AN OPEN MIND

Dear Lord, I pray that as I continue in Your Word, You will grant to me an open mind, one that will allow Your Word to feed my inner person with the bread of life.

Father, I realize I was a slave to sin and You called me out of sin. Lord Jesus, You called me out of sin and have now set me free from the awful power of sin, and now I am a slave to You.

Father, I vow, no matter what situation I find myself in, now that I am a believer, I am going to stay in this new relationship with Jesus, and nothing can separate me from Your love.

Father, I pray that You will transform me, by the renewing of my mind, that I will have the same mind that was in Christ Jesus. Then I will become one of Your disciples indeed; and I will know the truth, and the truth will make me free.

I realize I was born a slave to sin and now have received freedom. I'm referring to Spiritual freedom, now I am able to receive the truth and act upon it.

Father, I pray that I will not be so full of myself, that I can't respect the teachings of those You have placed over me.

Help me to respect the truth and not shut my mind to Your Word, even if I don't like what the truth says.

Father, I pray that You give me an open mind to the bitter parts of Your Word, though it may be unpleasant to me, as to the parts that are pleasant to me, because both are for my good.

Father, I praise You, for now I am standing fast in liberty, because Christ has made me free, and I am no longer entangled in the yoke of bondage.

In Jesus' Name I pray,

Amen

FOR ANXIETY

Father, I pray that when the Chief Shepherd appears, I will receive the crown of glory that will never fade away. I pray for a pure heart so I will be submissive and humble when it comes to humility toward others, because "You oppose the proud but give grace to the humble."

Father, I therefore humble myself under Your mighty hand, that You may lift me up in due time. I cast all my anxiety on You because You care for me.

Father, You know the weight and anxiety that oppresses me. Help me to bare it. Therefore, I also pray for self-control and alertness so I will believe I have no anxiety. Father, Your Word says be anxious for nothing.

Father, when the Lord Jesus Christ was on earth, He told me not to take anxiety into tomorrow, because You, my heavenly Father know the thing I need, and that You would take care of me.

Father, help me rest in Your Word, for You know what is necessary for me, and those who depend on me. Father, I pray that You give me the fullness of heaven, which is Yours to give.

Father, I thank You for delivering me from this anxiety that drains my energy in order to keep me unfit and unable to perform my duties to You. Lord Jesus, thank You for building my confidence so Your power can bring me through.

Father, I praise You, for now I am standing fast in liberty, because Christ has made me free, and I am no longer entangled in this yoke of bondage.

In Jesus' Name I pray,

Amen

FOR APPROACHING DEATH

Merciful Father, I pray that You will be with me in my last hours leading up to my death. I claim Your promise in 2 Corinthians 5:8.

Father, I am fully confident that when it's my time to die, that being away from this body, means being at home with You, Father.

Father, You made dying easy for me by sending Jesus Christ, my Lord, and Savior, who broke the power of death and showed me the way to everlasting life. Because my body is made of flesh and blood Lord You also became flesh and blood by being born in human form.

For only as a human being could You die, and only by dying could You break the power of the devil, who had the power to cause death. Only in this way could the Lord Jesus Christ, deliver me from a life of a slave to the fear of dying in my flesh.

Father, I praise You for comforting me and for the assurance that You are always present with me and for blessing me by forgiving all my sins. I pray that You will keep me Yours as the Holy Spirit preserves me until Jesus comes back to carry me home to Your awaiting arms.

Father, I realize that bodily death is not the end of my existence, but just a change of place and conditions. The Bible teaches that I am more than a physical creature, but a Spiritual being first. In His resurrection, the Lord Jesus Christ conquered physical death, Spiritually, and eternally.

Father, I Praise You, for now I am standing fast in liberty, because Christ has made me free, and I am no longer entangled in the yoke of bondage.

In Jesus' Name I pray,

Amen

FOR AUTHORITY ON LOOSING GOD'S BLESSINGS

I pray to You, O Lord the glorious Father of my Lord Jesus Christ, to give me Spiritual Wisdom, and understanding, so that I will grow in the knowledge of Jesus Christ.

I pray that my heart will be flooded with light so that I can understand the wonderful future You have promised to me who You called.

Father, I know the plans You have for me. "They are plans for good and not for evil, to give me a future and a hope. Father, when I pray, You will listen, and when I seek You, I will find You, if I look for You in earnest.

Yes, I will find You, and You will end my slavery and restore my fortunes, and gather me out of the wilderness, and bring me back home again to Your land.

Father, I pray, for You to help me to realize what a rich and glorious inheritance You have given to me

Lord I pray that I will begin to understand the incredible greatness of Your power that's available to us who believe in You. This is the same mighty power that raised Christ from the dead and seated Him in the place of honor at Your right hand in the heavens.

Now Jesus Christ is far above any ruler or authority or power or leader or anything else in this world or in the world to come.

And You, O Lord have put all things under the authority of Jesus Christ, and gave Him this authority for the benefit of me, "Halleluiah."

And I am a part of His Body; I am filled by Jesus Christ, who fills everything everywhere with His presence.

In Jesus' Name I pray,

Amen

MIGHTY MAN OF VALOR

Father, I have fixed my thoughts on what is true, honorable, and right. Holy Spirit, thank You for making me think about things that are pure, lovely and admirable. Lord Jesus, it's because of You that I think about things that are excellent and worthy of praise.

Thank You, Holy Spirit, for helping me to keep putting into practice all I have learned and heard from the Father and now the Lord's peace is with me. How grateful I am and how I praise You, Father, because You are concerned about me. Father, I know You have always been concerned for me.

Father, for a time I didn't give You the chance to help me, not that I thought I didn't need of Your help. For I have learned, to get along happily whether I have much or little, I need Your blessing. Lord, I pray for You to teach to learn the secret of living in every situation, whether it is with a full stomach or empty, with plenty or little. For I can do all things with the help of Christ who gives me the strength I need.

Almighty Father, I praise You, for You have made me the head and not the tail, the first and not last, the top and not the bottom, the "A" and not the "Z."

Lord, because of Your grace, I have victory in the work

that I do.

I give You thanks for making my life a successful one. Lord I thank You, for sending and angel to continue to remind me that You are with me because I am a Mighty Man of Valor.

Father, I thank You, for always being with me, I cannot fail because You have made me a Mighty Man Of Valor. My enemies cannot stand against the strength and courage You have given me, because I am a Mighty Man of Valor.

Father, I give You Praises, for I am a Mighty Man of Valor when it comes to my health and my wealth. I am a Mighty Man of Valor when it comes to faith and its' power. I am a Mighty Man of Valor when it comes to being a Valiant Man and a Man of War for You are always with me.

Lord, You have made me a ruler over all things, my household included. I am a ruler over the earth. Father, You have made me an honorable man because You have made Your home in me. Lord I dedicate my Life to only You.

Lord, because Your goodness endured continually in me, I am a Mighty Man of Valor when it comes to raising my children while they are in their youth.

I thank You, Lord, for You have made me a wise man of confidence, so that as I judge all things, I will be prudent because I am a prophet and a priest in my home.

Lord, as a Mighty Man of Valor I pray, that You will humble me.

Father, I pledge that as a Mighty Man of Valor, I shall do away with jealousy because I am a wise man; my glory rests in Your wisdom, so that none of the works I do shall be done in vain. Father, In Your wisdom I shall do mighty works.

Lord, I praise You because You have given me the victory by the authority of Your power to do all things, for all that is in heaven and in the Earth belong to You. Father, Yours is the Kingdom of God. You are exalted as head above all.

Now, the eye and the strength of my God is upon me and nothing can cause me to cease from praying and believing, till my life on Earth is completed.

In Jesus' Name I pray,

Amen

FOR BEING A PARENT

Father, I consider my children as a gift from You, and You have entrusted them to me for this short time. Father, I pray that You help me to be a worthy parent. Help me to train up my children in Your ways, Lord so when they are grown they will not depart from them.

Father, I pray that You will make me a good parent, and help me to receive these children You entrusted to me in Your name. Father, You said, who shall receive such little children In Your name receives You.

Father, I dedicate my children back to You and I pray that You make them strong in Your Spirit. Father, I pray that You send the Holy Spirit to give me wisdom, knowledge and understanding to help me know what Your Word teaches, concerning training children.

When I was a child, I spoke as a child, I understood as a child, I thought as a child, but when I became grown up, I put away childish things. Father, I pray that with Your guidance, I will supply my children with all the abilities necessary so when they are grown up they will be the son's and daughters of God.

Father, I pray that You will fill my heart with Your love and patience so I will be slow to discipline. Then I will not make my children angry by mistreating them or using inappropriate discipline. Father, help me bring them up with the discipline and instruction approved by You.

Father, Jesus clearly expressed His love and respect for children when He said. "Anyone who welcomes a little child on His behalf welcomes Him, and anyone who welcomes Him, welcomes His Father who sent Him." Father, I pray that like Jesus, I too will welcome all children at all times with the love of Jesus.

Father, give me Your wisdom and build my faith, then I will fully understand that my children resemble me and take on several of my qualities, good or bad. Father, make me a parent You will be proud of.

In Jesus' Name I pray,

Amen

VIRTUOUS PRINCESS

Lord I have fixed my thoughts on what is true, honorable, and right. Holy Spirit, thank You for making me think about things that are pure and lovely and admirable. Lord Jesus, it's because of You that I think about things that are excellent and worthy of praise.

Thank You Holy Spirit, for helping me to keep putting into practice all that I have learned and heard from the Father, and now the Lord's peace is with me. How grateful I am, and how I praise You, Lord because You are concerned about me. Lord I know You have always and always will be concerned about me.

Lord for a time I didn't know just how much You could help me. Not that I thought I was not in need of Your help. Father, help me learned that to be happy whether I have much or less, I need Your blessing. Lord teach me the secret of living in every situation, whether it is with a full stomach or an empty stomach, with plenty or little. For I can do everything with the help of Christ who gives me the strength I need.

Lord because of Your grace I have victory in every thing that I do. I give You thanks for making my life a successful one. Lord, send Your messenger angels to me, so they can continue to remind me, that You are always with me, because I am a Virtuous Princess.

Lord I thank You, for You are with me, and I cannot fail because You have made me a Virtuous Princess. And my enemies cannot stand against the strength and courage You have given me, because I am a Virtuous Princess.

I give You praise, Lord for I am a Virtuous Princess when it comes to my health, and my wealth. I am a Virtuous Princess when it comes to faith and power. I am a Virtuous Princess when it comes to being a valiant princess and a Virtuous Princess when I am at war with my flesh, because You are always with me.

Lord You have made me the ruler over all things. Because I am a ruler over the whole earth. Father, You have made me an honorable Virtuous Princess, because You have made my heart Your home. Lord I dedicate my life to only You always.

Lord because Your goodness endured continually in me, I am a Virtuous Princess.

I thank You, Lord for You have made me a wise Virtuous Princess with confidence, and so as I judge all things, I will be prudent because I am a Virtuous Princess. Lord as a Virtuous Princes, I pray that You will always keep me humble.

Lord I pledge that as a Virtuous Princess, I shall do away with jealousy because I am a wise Virtuous Princess. Lord my glory rests in Your wisdom, and I know that the works I do will not be done in vain. Father, In Your wisdom I will do mighty works.

Lord I praise You because You have given me the victory, with authority in Your power to do all things, for all that is in the heavens and in the Earth belongs to You. For Yours Is the kingdom of God. O Lord my Father, You are exalted as head above all.

Lord thank You for calling me Your daughter and now all people will know that I am a Virtuous Princess. Lord I praise You, for now I am standing fast in liberty, because Christ has made me free.

In Jesus' Name I pray,

Amen

VIRTUOUS WOMAN

Father, I have fixed my thoughts on what is true, honorable, and right. Holy Spirit, thank You for making me to think about things that are pure, lovely, and admirable. Lord Jesus, it's because of You that I think about things that are excellent and worthy when I praise the Lord my God.

Thank You, Holy Spirit, for helping me to keep putting into practice all I have learned and heard from the Father and now the Lord's peace is with me. How grateful I am and how I praise You, Lord because You are concerned about me. Father, I know You have always been concerned for me.

Father, for a time I didn't give You the chance to help me, not that I thought I didn't need of Your help. For I have learned that as long as I walk in Your Spirit, I can be happy and blessed, whether I have much or little. I have learned the secret of living in every situation, whether it is with a full stomach or empty, with plenty or little. For I can do all things with the help of Christ who gives me the strength I need.

Almighty Father, I praise You, for You have made me the head and not the tail. Thank You, heavenly Father, for You have made me first and not last, the top and not the bottom.

Lord, because of Your grace I have victory in the work

that I do. I give You thanks for making my life a successful one. Lord You sent an angel to remind me, that You are always with me, because I am a Virtuous Woman in Christ.

Father, I thank You, for You are with me and I cannot fail because You have made me a Virtuous Woman. My enemies cannot stand against the strength and courage You have given me, because I am a Virtuous Woman.

Father, I give You praise, because I am a Virtuous Woman when it comes to my health and my wealth. I am a Virtuous Woman when it comes to faith and its power. I am a Virtuous Woman when it comes to being a valiant woman and a woman of war for You are always with me.

Lord, You have made me a ruler over many things. I am a ruler over the Earth. Father, You have made me an honorable woman because You have made Your abode in me. Lord I dedicate my life to only You.

Lord, because Your goodness endured continually in me, I am a Virtuous Woman when it comes to raising my children while they are in their youth.

I thank You, Lord, for You have made me a wise woman of confidence, so as I judge all things, I will be prudent because

I am a Virtuous Woman. Lord as a Virtuous Woman, I pray You humble me.

Father, I pledge that as a Virtuous Woman, I will do away with jealousy because I am a wise woman. Lord my glory rests in Your wisdom so that none of the works I do will be done in vain. Father, in Your wisdom I will do mighty works.

Lord, I praise You because You have given me the victory, by the authority of Your power to do all things, for all that is in the heavens and in the Earth belongs to You. For Yours is The Kingdom of Heaven. O Lord You are exalted as head above all.

Lord, thank You for calling me Your daughter, and now all people know that I am a Virtuous Woman and that I am a crown to my husband. For You said, who finds a Virtuous Woman finds a good thing, for my price is far above rubies.

Father, I Praise You for now I am standing fast in liberty, because Christ has made me free and I am no longer entangled in the yoke of bondage.

In Jesus' Name I pray,

Amen

FOR CHEERFULNESS

Merciful Father, who set the standards on being cheerful, make me cheerful so I can always praise Your Holy name. Father, help me to always believe with my whole heart, that You have always loved me, Father, help me to know that all things work together for good to them that love You, and for us who are the called according to Your purpose.

Father, help me to always praise Your Holy name. Lord help me to always tell myself to never forget the good things You have done for me. How You forgive all my sins and heal all my diseases. How You have ransomed me from death and surrounded me with Your love and tender mercies.

Father, help me remember that You always fill my life with good things, and that You renew my youth daily. Lord, help me to bring all my emotions, sorrows, and the experience of emotional distress and pains under subjection. Father, help me to always remember that I walk by faith, not by sight.

Father, help me to be able to talk only about the good and not the bad when I express what I feel in periods of intense sadness. Lord, don't let me be a "stumbling block" to those I love.

Father, help me to always remember, that there is hope in Christ, who "surely...has borne my grief's," all the way to the cross.

Lord, and the Father of my Lord and Savior Jesus Christ, when sorrow comes, help me to always remember that there is still joy in You, even while I am on Earth, and that in time, I shall experience happiness again and that I will spread happiness all around me.

"This is the day that the Lord has made and I will rejoice in it."

In Jesus' Name I pray,

Amen

THAT CHRIST MAY LIVE IN MY HEART

Father, when I think of the wisdom and scope of the plans that You have for me, I bow down on my knees and pray. Lord You are the Creator of everything in heaven and on earth and the Father of my Lord and Savior Jesus Christ, of whom the whole family in heaven and earth are named. Lord, I pray that from Your glorious, unlimited resources that You will build in me mighty inner strength through Your Holy Spirit.

Father, I pray for increased faith, so Christ will live in my heart and be more and more at home to help me trust in You. Father, I also pray that You make my roots to go down deep into the soil of Your marvelous love. Father, I pray for the power to understand, as all Your children should, just how wide, how long, how high, and how deep Your love really is.

Now unto Him that is able to do exceedingly abundantly above all that I ask or think according to the power that works in me,
Father, unto You be the glory in the church, through Christ Jesus Throughout all ages world without end.
In Jesus' Name I pray,
Amen

FOR COMFORT

Father, I pray in Jesus name for Your perfect peace, Your comfort, and that I will be of one mind, so I will live in peace. And that You, the Father of love and peace, will always be with me.

Dear Father in heaven, who's the Lord of all comfort, pour into my heart Your peace and strength. Father, the storms of life have over taken me. I have been beaten down and utterly discouraged.

My soul faints within me. My sorrow is greater than I can bear. I am too weak for the burden laid upon me. I pray to You, dear Lord, send me the comfort of Your presence.

Father, I pray, bring peace to my soul. Comfort me as a parent comforts his children. Hold me in Your arms of mercy.

Father, I praise You, for now I am standing fast in liberty, because Christ has made me free, and I am no longer entangled in the yoke of bondage.

Thank You, Lord.

In Jesus' Name I pray,

Amen

FOR CONVALESCENCE

(To grow strong, to be strong, and to recover health gradually)

Father, I always claim Your promises in 3rd John, verse 2, as I pray in Jesus name, that all is well with me and, that my body is as healthy as I know my soul is healthy.

Father, I always thank You for granting me relief from suffering, I pray that as I recover to perfect health that I will always give You praise and glory for being present with me in my hour of need.

Father, Your peace continues to calm me, as You keep me from being inpatient in this time of total recovery. Father, I pray for Your strength that it will make the words of my mouth and the meditation of my heart acceptable in Your sight. Father, as I recover I pray for You to help me keep my past suffering in the past, so it will not hinder You blessing me by my talking about it.

Father, I pray that out of Your abundance You will bless those who wait on me, and lighten their task, as You cheerfully reward them for their services to me.

Let the eye and strength of my Lord be upon me, so nothing can cause me to cease from praying and believing, till this matter is completed.

Father, I praise You, for now I am standing fast in liberty, because Christ has made me free, and I am no longer entangled in the yoke of bondage.

In Jesus' Name I pray,

Amen

FOR ENDURANCE

Father, You are the One who gives me the endurance to serve You and perform my Spiritual duties.

Father, I pray that You will help me be strong and bless me with more endurance, so I will be able to serve You better, and to bear the failings of those that are weaker than me.

Father, help me not look to always please myself but to please my neighbor in ways that will be for their good to help build them up.

Father, Jesus did not look to please Himself but He showed me that everything that was written in the past was written to teach me, so that through endurance and the encouragement of the Scriptures I might have hope.

Father, I pray that as You build in me endurance and encouragement teach my will to be in unity with Your Spirit, which lives in me and help me to follow the example that Jesus left.

Father, give me the same heart and mind that was in Jesus, and I will endure in my labors as I glorify You, Lord.

Father, just as the suffering Christ endured proved to be my comfort, so through Christ, make me endure my suffering, so it will prove to be comfort, as my endurance overflows into the life of others.

Father, I pray that You will help me to understand, that If I am distressed, it is for my comfort which produces salvation. If I am comforted, it is for my comfort, which produces in me endurance.

Father, strengthen me with all power according to Your glorious might, so that I will have great endurance and patience as I joyfully give thanks to You.

Father, help me to continually remember that my trials produced faith and that Your faith prompted by Your love produced endurance in me, inspired by hope in the Lord Jesus Christ.

Father, I pray, help me to always pursue righteousness, godliness, faith, love, endurance, and gentleness. Father, help me to always endure in the fruit of the Spirit, self-control, so I can fight the good fight of faith.

Father, teach me to be temperate, worthy of respect, and help me to be sound in faith, love, mind, and endurance.

Father, as a servant of Jesus Christ, I commend myself in every way for great endurance in troubles, hardships distresses and suffering, that I will exercise the patience and endurance that are mine in Jesus.

In Jesus' Name I pray,

Amen

FOR FAIRNESS

Dear Lord, who is the judge of all the Earth, please give me the grace of Your fairness. Then I will spring from the stem of Jesus, and then as a branch from His roots I will bear fruit, and the Spirit of the Lord will rest on me; the Spirit of wisdom and understanding, the Spirit of counsel and strength, the Spirit of knowledge and the fear of the Lord.

And I will delight in the fear of the Lord and I will not judge by what my eyes see, nor make a decision by what my ears hear.

But with righteousness I will judge the poor, and decide with fairness for the afflicted of the earth. Father, make righteousness the belt about my loins, and faithfulness the belt about my waist.

Father, help me to proceed with my duty of being a servant to You. Not only with my justice, but with strict equity and kindness. Father, help me to deal with others as I expect You should deal with me.

Lord, don't let my feelings carry me into thinking that wrong is right. Help me to make allowances for circumstances, and not to condemn hastily.

In Jesus' Name I pray, Amen

FOR FAITH

Father, there are many things that I do not understand. I pray that You will reveal to me the true meaning of Your Word, so I will know what You meant when You said to me, "if I would do Your will, I must first deny self, and pick up my own cross and follow You".

Father, I pray in Jesus' name, as I crucify my flesh daily, that You will grant me a double dose of Your wisdom. I also pray that You will give me an understanding as I read Your Word.

Father, then I will know without doubt that faith is the substance of things hoped for and the evidence of things I cannot see, and what so-ever I pray for will take place.

Father, I pray that as I come talking with You, I will always come believing that You are the Father of my Lord and Savior, Jesus Christ, the originator of my faith.

Father, I pray that You build my faith so I that I will know without a doubt, "You reward me as I sincerely seek You," because the Bible says in Heb 11:6, that it is impossible to please You without faith. Holy Spirit, build my faith.

Father, help me to live so that I may have the knowledge that is needed for me to live in Your Word. Help me to follow in the footsteps of Jesus Christ, and not be troubled about questions of belief. I pray daily that as I live my life, it will show that I have faith in You. Because I know that as I enter into Your Kingdom, all mysteries will be made clear to me.

    Father, please grant me the strength in Your light to walk by faith, so that the Holy Spirit might lead me into all truth.

In Jesus' Name I pray,

Amen

FOR FORGIVENESS

Father, out of the depths have I cried unto You, O Lord hear my voice: let Your ears be attentive to the words of my supplications. Father, if You should hold me accountable for all my iniquities, O Lord how shall I stand, but there is forgiveness within You.

Father, as one of Your children, who is called by Your name, I come before You, humbling myself, and praying, and seeking Your face.

Father, help me to turn from my wicked ways, Father, I pray, that You will hear my cry from heaven, and forgive my sin, and heal all of me.

Father, when I was a sinner You saved me, You forgave every kind of sin that I ever committed. Father, because of the blood of Jesus Christ, You still forgive my sins, now help me to always seek Your face when I am faced with the decision, to or not to forgive others.

Father, even when I have committed a terrible sin, when I return back to You, Lord, You forgive me. Father, I pray help me to be able to transform Your forgiving me, to me forgiving others.

Father, if another believer sins against me, Your Word says to rebuke them, and then if they repent, forgive them. Even if they wrong me seven times a day, and each time turns to me and asks for my forgiveness, Father, increase my faith to help me forgive them in love, every time.

Father, I also pray, please forgive others for their sins against You, me and each other. Father, help us to worship You together.

Father, I thank You for opening my eyes, and turning me from darkness to light, and from the power of Satan. Lord help me receive and give forgiveness.

Father, I pray, soften my heart, so I will do others no harm by word or deed. If bitter thoughts are in my mind and cruel words come to my lips, help me to suppress them. Father, thank You for redeeming me through the blood of Jesus for the forgiveness of all sin.

In Jesus' Name I pray,

Amen

FOR FAITHFULNESS

Father, I thank You for making faithfulness one of the characteristics of Your loving nature. For it denotes the firmness of Your loyalty in Your relations with Your children.

Father, I praise You because You are the Lord of truth, and of unchangeableness. Father, You are constant and faithful in keeping Your promises, and therefore are worthy of all my trust.

Father, I know that all goodness, mercy, and loyalty are parts of Your covenant promises, and I thank You for having chosen me to be great in Your faithfulness.

Father, I pray that You send the Holy Spirit, so He will change me by taking out my old heart and replace it with a new heart - one capable of receiving Your impressions, so I will be a faithful witness of You to others.

Lord, thank You for giving me a work to do while I am on this Earth. Help me to be a "faithful witness" and a "faithful servant." Lord, clothe me with Your faithfulness and deliver me from temptation.

Father, I realize that Your faithfulness is the source of my deliverance from temptations and the assurance of my salvation. Help me give my faithfulness back to You in the very best service I can.

Father, I thank You that Your faithfulness is so deeply reflected in me, and that You have forgiven all of my sins. My prayer is that You make me faithful to You, and help me to forgive all that may have sinned against me.

Praise every one the Lord for the eye and strength of my God is upon me, and nothing can cause me to cease from praying and staying faithful, till the day of the Lord. Christ has made me free, because the yoke of bondage has been lifted.

In Jesus' Name I pray,

Amen

FOR FRANKNESS

Father, I pray, that Your love may abound in me, yet more and more in knowledge and in all judgment.

Father, I pray, for You to help me to always approve of the things that are excellent, and disapprove of the things that are not of You. I pray that I will always be sincere and without offense till the day Christ comes for me.

Father, I pray that You will fill me with the fruits of the Spirit, Righteousness, which is through Jesus Christ, unto the glory and Praise of You Lord. Father, help me to be frank and to the point when it comes to what is right.

Father, I pray, help me approve of the things that are excellent, and not be afraid to search out things that differ". Father, help me to realize there are some things that differ one from other; as morality and grace, earthly things, and Heavenly things, carnal and Spiritual, temporal and Eternal things, law and Gospel, the doctrines of men, and the Doctrines of Christ.

Father, I pray, teach me Your ways, because Your ways differ from my ways as much as gold, silver, and precious stones, differ from wood, hay and stubble.

Father, help me to be transformed, by the renewing of my mind, and bless me with spiritual insight and knowledge.

And bless me with Your spiritual senses as I discern the difference between all things.

Father, with Spiritual judgment and sense, all of my advice to others will be honest, sincere, and frank as Christ gives me knowledge. Lord help me to hate deceit. Make me frank and open in my dealings with others.

Lord, make me careful of the feelings of those to whom I have to speak. If there are unpleasant things that must be said, let me soften the words as much as possible.

Father, bless my frankness and never let it cause pain, or shame, to You, and keep me from saying anything that I would not like said to me.

In Jesus' Name I pray,

Amen

FOR GAINING WEALTH

Father, I will always remember that You are my Lord and my God, every time I give You Praise. For it is You who has given me the power to get wealth. Father, it was You who established Your covenant when You swore unto my father's fathers.

Lord, You said to them, "Always remember, it is I, the Lord, for I am the one who gives you the power to get wealth." That same covenant remains till this day.

Father, it was You who led them through that great and terrible wilderness, wherein there were fiery serpents, scorpions, droughts and no water. Father, You brought them forth water out of the rock. Father, it was You who fed them in the wilderness with manna.

Father, I pray first and foremost that You bless me with spiritual wealth and wisdom. Father, I pray and ask above all that You give me an understanding. Then as You bless me with physical wealth, I will have the power to be a good steward and therefore give You praise as I consecrate the use of it.

Father, You gave to me the same Holy Spirit with all of Your attributes and abilities that were available to the Lord Jesus Christ while He walked the Earth.

Father, I pray, help me to be able to activate all of the mighty works of Your Holy Spirit, so I can cross every fear and mountain that may get in my way.

Father, put in me a heart in the likeness of the heart Solomon had, so that I will not use the riches and wealth You bless me with, for self honor.

Father, Your word says, "Blessed is the man that fears You, that delights greatly in Your commandments. His seed shall be mighty upon Earth; and all his generations shall be blessed."

Father, I claim Your promises where You said that wealth and riches should be in my house and that Your righteousness endures forever. Father, help me to live upright and live in the light and not in the darkness.

Father, give me the ability to earn it honestly and to spend it wisely.

In Jesus' Name I pray,

Amen

FOR GOD'S FULL BLESSINGS

Father, for this cause I bow down on my knees unto You, the Father of my Lord Jesus Christ. Of whom the whole family in heaven and earth is named.

Father, that You would grant me, according to the riches of Your glory, to be strengthened in Your might by Your Spirit, to strengthen my soul.

Father, I praise You for sending Christ to live in my heart by faith, now I am rooted and grounded in Your love. Now I am able to comprehend with all the saints what is the breadth, and length, and depth, and height; and to know the love of Christ, who passes knowledge, that I will be filled with all the fullness of You, Lord.

Now unto the Lord who is able to do exceeding abundantly above all that I ask or think, according to the power that works in me,

Unto the Lord be the glory in the church by Christ Jesus throughout all ages, world without end.

In Jesus' Name I pray,

Amen

FOR GOD'S WISDOM

Lord, by Your wisdom You founded the earth, by Your understanding You established the heavens, by Your knowledge the depths were broken up and the skies drip with dew.

Lord, with Your wisdom I can build a house, with Your understanding I can establish it; With Your Knowledge I can fill the rooms with precious and pleasant riches.

Lord, help me to do Your will, make me wise and strengthen me. Lord I pray, fill me in Your knowledge and increased power. Lord, with Your wise guidance, I can wage war against my flesh, and get the victory.

Lord You gave wisdom to Solomon, just as You promised him, and all the Earth was seeking the presence of Solomon, to hear his wisdom, which You put in his heart, mind, and soul.

Father, You said to Solomon, because he asked for wisdom and did not asked for himself long life, or for riches or the death of his enemies. Instead he asked for himself discernment to understand Your justice. Lord, You gave Solomon wisdom, great discernment, and depth of mind. Solomon's wisdom surpassed the wisdom of all the sons of Egypt.

Father, I pray that You will give me, Your servant, that same wisdom, and understanding as Solomon.

And Lord, I pray, mold my heart to judge all people, with Your wisdom, and then I will be able to discern the differences between good and evil.

Father, in Jesus' name, I pray, as did Solomon, not for riches and honor, are even for long life. Rather I pray, Father, give me a heart capable of discernment, and then I will understand Your justice.

Father, as You did unto Moses, educate me and teach me the power of Your Words and deeds.

Father, as Your servant David walked before You in truth, righteousness, and uprightness of heart, You reserved for Him, and he displayed great loving kindness to others.

Father, I pray in the Lord Jesus Christ's name, that You reserve for me the same great loving kindness, and put Your wisdom in my heart and fill me with Your Holy Spirit so I can walk before You in truth, righteousness, and uprightness of heart.

Father, I pray that You grant me Your wisdom so I will find peace in all my dealings. Lord, grant me wisdom so I can live in the light of Your presence, just as Christ did.

Lord, give me the wisdom I need to guide my children during their years in my care.

Father, raise me up as an instrument capable of doing Your special work in their lives. And Father, teach me to show them how to go out or come in, and to discern between good and evil.

Lord, I praise You for building my children's faith and sending the gift of healing so they will be able to remain healthy.

Father, grant me Your grace of wisdom. Father, make me wise enough to choose truth over falsehood. Lord, I pray for Your knowledge of salvation, and thank You for forgiveness of my sins. Your tender mercy will live forever.

In Jesus' Name I pray,

Amen

FOR GRATITUDE

My Father, who lives in heaven, Lord, You are the originator of my expectation, my joy and the hope of my eternal salvation. I praise You because You are the source of everything that I enjoy and because all good things come from You.

Father, I pray that You will fill my heart with gratitude towards You. Father, don't let ungratefulness be in my heart. Father, help me to endure as You develop the strength of Your character in me.

Father, I pray that You will send the Holy Spirit to strengthen my confidence and expectation of salvation. Father, I know You will not disappoint me, for I know how dearly You love me. Thank You for filling my heart with Your love.

Father, when I was utterly helpless, You sent Jesus at just the right time to die for my sins. And Father, You showed how great You love me, by sending Him while I was still a sinner.

Father, I pray as I receive gifts from You, I will always show pleasure in them and not receive them as though they were a right.

Father, when You show special favor to me, or to those I love, help me to express my gratitude fully and honestly. And let my gratitude satisfy those who have been generous to me.

Father, You give good gifts, I pray for You to help me show You that I am truly grateful to You.

Now the eye and strength of my God is upon me, so nothing can cause me to cease from praying and believing, till this life is completed.

Father, I praise You, for now I am standing fast in liberty, because Christ has made me free, and I am no longer entangled in the yoke of bondage.

In Jesus' Name I pray, Amen

FOR HAPPINESS

O Lord, bend down Your ear, and hear my prayer; answer me, for I need Your help. Protect me, for I am devoted to You. Save me, for I serve You and trust You. You are my God, be merciful, O Lord, for I am calling on You constantly for happiness.

Father, help me to love my enemies, and to do good to those who hate me. Father, help me to pray for the happiness of those who curse me, and those who hurt me.

O Lord, I pray, give me Your happiness, for my life depends on You. Lord, You are so good, so ready to forgive, so full of happiness and unfailing love for all who ask Your aid.

O Lord, listen closely to my prayer, hear my urgent cry. Father, I will call to You whenever trouble strikes and You will answer me, and give me happiness.

Father, discipline me when needed, for it brings me happiness and peace of mind. Father, I pray, help me give pleasure a try. Father, help me to look for the good things in life along with happiness.

Father, after much thought, I decided to cheer for myself, while I am still seeking wisdom, I will clutch at foolishness.

Lord in this way, I hoped to experience the only true happiness most people never find during their brief life in this world. My happiness is in You.

Father, Jesus said, "You bless those who are poor, and that Your Kingdom belongs to them. And that You bless those that are hungry, and satisfy them. Jesus also said, "You bless those who weep, for the time will come when they will laugh with joy, Yes, leap for joy! For a great reward waits them in heaven.

Heavenly Father, thank You for filling my heart with this overflowing happiness, Lord help me to know that all of this goodness has come from You.

In Jesus' Name I pray,

Amen

OUR FAMILY PRAYER

Good morning Holy Spirit, Father, my family and I come at this time to lift up the name of the Lord, to give You praise, to give You honor, and to give You glory, because You alone are worthy to be praised.

Father, this is the day that the Lord has made and I will rejoice and be glad in it. Father, I lift up my family banner declaring Your praise. Thank You, Father, for keeping and blessing my family and me, not only today, but each and every day.

Father, these are my family records, as descendants of Adam. On the day that You created us, You made us in Your image and Your likeness and I give You the highest praise.

Father, these are my family records, like Abraham, I pray daily that You make us a righteous family - one that holds one another up in prayer daily. Father, make us a family that is blameless among our contemporaries and help us to always want to walk with You.

Father, these are the family records of our sons and daughters. Father, I pray as they strive to walk with You, that You will send Your angels with them and make their journey a success.

Father, help us each and every morning to present ourselves one by one as we come forward and repent our faults one to another and before You daily.

Father, help us show family affection to one another with brotherly love and help each to outdo the other in showing honor to each other.

Father, we pray that You will show us how to be rooted and firmly established in love for one another and to know the God kind of love that surpasses knowledge, so we may be filled with all Your fullness.

In Jesus' Name I pray,

Amen

FOR HONORING PARENTS

Father, Your Word teaches children to honor our father and mother, so that we will live a long, full life in the land the Lord our Father will give us. Father, I pray that You will help me to submit to the authority my parents have over me.

Father, while the law gave my parents full authority over me for as long as I am under their care, it also provided against the abuse of that authority. Lord, as my parents provide nurturing and guidance during my childhood years, I pray that You will help them to honor their parental duties, and help me to obey them fully, as well.

Father, help me to always show respect for my father and mother, as well as all of my elders, even when I am no longer a child. Father, Your Word teaches that parents have the responsibility of loving their children in the way Jesus loved children. Lord help me to love my parents as Jesus loves me.

Father, in the New Testament, Paul instructed parents to bring up their children in the training and admonition of the Lord. Father, show my parents Your perfect will for my life, and help them to carry it out.

Father, I pray that You teach me how to choose the right path, and how to remain upon it. And Father, help me to work hard so You will approve of me, and help me to be a good worker, one who does not need to be ashamed and who correctly explains the Word of Truth.

In Jesus' Name I pray,

Amen

FOR HOPE

Father, I pray in Jesus' name that You will fill my heart with Your Joy so that my mouth will continue to shout Your Praises!

Heavenly Father, I pray for You to grant me the gift of hope, for my life is dark and full of sorrow. At times, it seems that there is nothing to look forward to but more sadness and disappointment.

Father, I pray that my body will always rest in the hope that You will not leave my soul among the dead, or allow me to rot in the grave.

Father, I pray that You show me that life has duties and many pleasures still waiting for me. Father, place within me the desire to live, plant hope in my heart that despairs may vanish as the dew before the sun.

I know all good things come from You, and You have promised to give them to me, one of Your children who is trying to serve You. Send Your hope and happiness to me, that it may brighten my way.

Now the eye and strength of my Lord is upon me, so nothing can cause me to cease from praying and believing, till the matter is completed.

Father, I praise You, for now I am standing fast in liberty, because Christ has made me free, and I am no longer entangled in the yoke of bondage.

In Jesus' Name I pray,

Amen

FOR HUMILITY

Eternal God, my Father, who despises the proud and gives grace to the humble, give me the grace of Your humility.

Father, I am a prisoner in service to the Lord Jesus Christ. Father, I pray, help me to lead a life worthy of my calling, for I have been called by You, Lord.

Father, help me to be humble to others, situations, circumstances, and to be gentle, and patient at all times, as I learn how to make allowance for other's faults because of Your love.

Father, I pray, help me to always strive to keep my self-united in the Holy Spirit, and bind my self together with Your peace, and the humility of the Lord Jesus Christ.

Father, Jesus said that we are all one body, we have the same Spirit, and we have all been called to the same glorious future.

Father, I pray in Jesus name, help me to really know that there is only one Lord one faith, one baptism, and there is only one God and Father, who is over me and is living Your will through me.

Father, since You chose me to be a Holy person whom You can love, I pray that You clothe me with the same tenderhearted mercy, kindness, humility, gentleness and patience that the Lord Jesus Christ displayed.

Lord, teach me how to make allowances for other's faults and forgive any person who offends me. And teach me not to remember.

Father, You forgave me. I pray, help me forgive others. Father, I pray, help me to always understand that the most important piece of clothing I must wear is love. Father, Your Word teaches that love is what binds us all together in perfect harmony. Lord, Your Word also teaches that I must always let the peace that comes from Christ rule in my heart.

For as a member of His body, I am called to live in peace and to always be thankful.

Father, help me to always be honest in my estimate of myself, help me to always measure my self-value by the faith You have given me.

Father, Your Word teaches that my body has many parts and each part has a special function, and so it is with Christ's body. And that I am part of His body where each member has different work to do.

And that since we are all one body in Christ, we belong to each other, and each of us needs all of the others.

Father, the Bible says that You have given each of us the ability to love one another in the same manor that Jesus loves us.

Eternal God, my Father, who despises the proud and gives grace to the humble, give me the grace of Your humility.

In Jesus' Name I pray,

Amen

FOR KEEPING ME TODAY

Father, I pray this day for Your special blessings. I pray that You keep and protect me and my family through out this day. Father, I pray that You always smile on my family and are gracious to us.

Lord, I pray that You show my family and me Your favor and give us Your peace throughout this day. Father, You are rich in favor and full in blessings. Father, help me to be consistent in my walk, as I follow You so I can enjoy a closer relationship with You.

Father, I pray, bless everywhere my family and I go and bless everyone we come in contact with today. Lord, I pray that You will be with us and grant us Your special favor, even in the midst of our enemies.

Holy Spirit, with Your help, I will serve the Father completely today. Father, I pray in Jesus' name that as I please You, You will call me by my name and tell me You have found favor in me. Holy Spirit, help me to make all the right choices today so I will please the Lord, my God, completely.

Father, I pray, that You will reveal in my spirit, Your prefect will for me today, and make me to understand You fully so I will know exactly what You want from me today. Father, never let me forget that all good gifts I have come from You.

Lord, I pray that You will go with me every where I go today, then I will know that everything will work out just fine. Father, if I try to go anyplace or do anything You do not approve of, Lord, my prayer is You stop me. Father, I only want to go and do the things that will be pleasing to You. Father, then I will see Your glorious presence in everything I do today.

Father, I thank You, and I praise the Lord with all my heart, with all my soul and with all my strength. Father, I will testify to every one of all the marvelous things You have done for me and my family, not only today, but every day. Lord, I am filled with joy because of Your love. I will sing praises to Your name, for You have refused to let my enemy's triumph over me. My future is in Your hands.

Father, all that I am now, is all because You poured out Your special favor on me, but not without results, for I am now working harder than I have ever worked before on my Christian walk. Yet, it is not I, but God the Father, God the Son and God the Holy Spirit, who are working through me by Your grace. This is the day that the Lord has made, and I will rejoice and be glad in it. In Jesus' Name I pray, Amen

LET GO AND LET GOD

Father, Your entire existence to me is based on my faith in You. Your Word says, "It is impossible to please You without faith." Anyone who wants to come to You must believe that You are God and that You reward those who sincerely seek You in all things.

Father, You gave this warning: You said to me, "Be honest in my estimate of myself and that I should measure my faith not by how much faith You have given me but by how much faith I have now."

Father, help me to believe that You are the God of the Bible and that You do reward me when I sincerely seek You in all things. Father, help me to know when to let go of a situation and give it to You. Father, teach me how let go and let God. Father, teach me how to leave what I let go of and gave to You, with You.

In Jesus' Name I pray,

Amen

FOR LIFTING UP MY FAMILY

Our Father, who lives in heaven, may Your name be honored, may Your kingdom come soon. Father, may Your will be done here on Earth, just as it is in heaven.

Father, Jesus said, "And I, if I be lifted up from the Earth, I will draw all people unto myself." Father, I pray, for You to show me how to always lift up You and my Lord and Savior, Jesus Christ.

Father, Jesus assured me, that if I have faith and don't doubt, I would do things like He did and much more." I can even say to any mountain, in Jesus name, "Be lifted up and cast into the sea and it will happen."

Father, Your Word says, "When I bow down before You, confess my faults and depend on You, and You will lift me up and give me honor.

Father, right now, in the name of Jesus, I lift up my family in prayer. Father, I declare that all things in my household come into agreement with Your perfect will.

Father, in the mighty name of Jesus, I speak provision, health and prosperity over everyone under my roof.

Father, I pray that all family members will stand to attention and be able to hear the voice of the Lord clearly. Father, I pray for complete and utter victory over any and all challenges being faced by my family.

By the authority given to me by the Father, through the Son and the Holy Spirit, in Jesus' name, I command all enemies on assignment against my family to be loosed from your assignment and I bind you up. I cast you down and out and I drive you away from my family.

Father, I declare that all assignments of evil against my family be broken by the blood of Jesus! I demand that all demonic activity against my family be nullified and void against us.

Father, in the powerful name of Jesus, I pray that all members of my family be stable, healthy, unified and energized through Your Holy Spirit.

Come forth, Holy Spirit of the Living God and have Your way in each of our lives this day and every day thereafter.

Father, help all of us serve you with our whole lives. Help all of us recognize that You are Lord!

Father, help all of us receive the blessings that You desire to give each of us.

Father, give us strength, give us revelation, give us hope and give us peace. Father, give us unity. Father, fill our needs.

In Jesus' Name I pray, Amen

FOR AUTHORITY IN LOOSING AND BINDING

Father, I pray in Jesus name that above all things I will prosper and be in health, even as my soul prospers.

Father, I pray that You approve of me and do all the good things You have promised, and revile in me all the plans You have for me. They are plans for good and not for evil, to give me a future and a hope.

Father, You said that when I pray, You will listen, and If I look for You in earnest, I will find You. Lord, teach me how to seek Your favor, and to end my captivity to my flesh. Father, I pray that You will restore my fortunes. And Father, gather me out of my iniquities, and bring me home again, back to Your house.

Father, I pray that You will give me the keys to the kingdom of heaven. And Lord, I claim Your promises in Matt. 16:18-19 where You said to me "assuredly, whatever I bind on earth will be bound in heaven, and whatever I loose on earth will be loosed in heaven."

Father, show me how to bind up all of the evil forces that are assigned to destroy the works You are performing in me. Father, in Jesus' name, I bind up all unwanted and evil spirits that have been assigned to destroy the works that the Lord is performing in me.

I cast out all unwanted spirits in Jesus name, and you will never be assigned to me again.

Father, I pray for You to show me how to loose the fruits of the Spirit that You have given me when I accepted Jesus Christ as Lord of my life.

Father, thank You for giving me the authority to loose the fruits of Your, Holy Spirit in to my life, as You loose from heaven Your Power in my behalf.

In Jesus' Name I pray,

Amen

FOR MAKING CORRECT DECISIONS

Father, You are the teacher of all things, Your wisdom surpasses all understanding. Lord, I pray that You will fill me with Your, Holy Spirit, and give me great wisdom along with Spiritual intelligence, and make me a master skilled in making all kinds of decisions.

Father, I pray for Your wisdom, and that You will teach me Your perfect will concerning the choices I make. Father, Your Word, says that if I ask You, You will gladly tell me, and that You will not resent my asking.

Father, help me build my faith to the point that when I ask You to help me make the right decision, I will be sure to wait on Your answer.

Father, help me not to be of a doubtful mind, and help me not to waver.

Father, fill me with the Holy Spirit, and give me great wisdom when it comes to making all decisions.

Father, give me an understanding mind so that I can know the difference between right and wrong. Father, You are the foundation of true wisdom.

Father, make my way clear before my eyes, that I may take the right path.

So much seems to depend on my decision, and I do not know how to decide, as I should. Father, teach me Your wisdom and discipline, and to help me to make a wise decision.

In Jesus' Name I pray,

Amen

THE LORD IS MY SHEPHERD I

Lord You are my shepherd, and You supply me with anything I need.

Lord, teach me how to lie down in green pastures, and teach me to let You lead me beside the still waters, which is for my eternal life.

Lord, I pray for You to restore my soul, and lead me in the path of righteousness for Your name's sake.

And Father, even though You allow me to walk through the valley of the shadow of death, I will fear no evil, for You are with me. Lord it is Your rod and Your staff that comfort me.

Lord You prepare the table before me even in the presence of my enemies. Lord You are the one who anoints my head with oil, and makes my cup to run over. Lord I thank You for taking care of me.

Surely, Your goodness and Your mercy will follow me all the days of my life, and I will dwell in Your house Lord forever.
In Jesus' Name I pray,
Amen

FOR MARRIED COUPLES

Father, during creation, as You completed each day's assignment, You said, "It was good". But when You saw that man was all alone, You said, "It is not good for man to be alone. I will make him a helper, one who is of himself."

Father, You took the rib along with all the female organs out of man and formed a woman and brought her back to him, so that one half would complete the other half again.

Father, You call one half man and one half woman, for woman was taken from man. Father, help us realize that we are bone-of-bone, flesh- of-flesh, and Spirit-of-Spirit. Father, help us to leave even our father and mother and bond with each other. Father, show us how to make the two halves become one flesh, one soul and one Spirit as we were in creation.

Father, the question is how we become a righteous spouse unless You change us. Father, we thank You for changing us into a righteous spouse. Father, make us promise to always remember our marriage covenant vow, "Till death do we part."

Father, Your Word says, when a man finds a bride he finds a good thing, and obtains favor from You.

Father, help us to give all our love to one another in the same manner that Jesus gives all His love to us. Lord we pray that You help us love each part because that makes us a whole person.

Father, we pray that You will help us to guard the house and riches that we receive from You as an inheritance and Father, we praise You for making each of us a prudent spouse, and we promise to take very good care of both of us. Father, we pray that You will guard our whole heart, body, and soul.

Father, You said that a righteous spouse is a crown to the other: Lord we thank You for making us a righteous spouse that's baptized in the blood of the Lamb, and help us not to bring shame into our home.

Father, we pray that You will help us to love You with all our heart, with all our soul, with all our might, and to love each half as Jesus loves the whole. Father, we will always give You all glory, all Praise, and Your entire honor, as we build our marriage to please You.

In Jesus' Name I pray,

Amen

FOR MARRIED (MAN)

Father, during creation, as You completed each day's assignment, You said, "It was good." But when You saw that man was all-alone, You said, "It is not good for the man to be alone." "I will make him a helper who is of himself." Father, You took the rib along with all the female organs out of the man and formed a woman and brought her to the man, so that one half would complete the other half again.

Father, help me realize that my wife is bone of my bone, flesh of my flesh, and Spirit of Spirit, for she was taken from me. Father, Your Word says this is why I shall leave my father and mother and bond with my wife, now our two halves have become one flesh, one soul, and one Spirit again. Lord help me bond with the Virtuous Woman in Christ, You sent me.

Father, the question is how can I find a virtuous woman? Unless she comes from You, for her price is far above rubies. Father, I thank You for blessing me with a virtuous wife, now Father help me love her in the same way that Christ loves me.

Father, Your Word says, when I found my wife I found a good thing, and obtained favor from You. Father, I pray for You to help me to treat my wife in the same manner that Jesus treats me.

Father, I pray that You will help me to guard the house and riches that I receive from You as an inheritance. Father, I praise You because You have given me a prudent wife. Now, I pray that You will able me to take very good care of her.

Father, help me to realize that this Virtuous Woman You sent me is my crown. Lord, thank You for sending me a wife that has been baptized in the blood of the Lamb for she brings honor into our home.

Father, I pray that You will teach me how to lead our home under the leadership of the Lord Jesus Christ and Father, help me to submit fully to Your Spiritual leadership.

Father, I pray that You will help me fulfill my marital duty to my wife. Lord help me to realize that I do not have authority over my own body but my wife does. Equally, help my wife realize that she does not have authority over her own body but I do. Father, help us to not deprive one another - except when we agree for a time, to devote ourselves to prayer. Lord help us to be of one mind and one Spirit.

Father, I pray that You will show me how to love You with all my heart, with all my soul, with all my strength, and to cherish my wife as Jesus loves me. Father, make me follow Your Word completely and to except the bitter parts of Your Word, as I accept the sweet parts.

Father, show me how to be strong and to remain on the wall that You and I are building. Father, if a time should come that my wife may be struggling in her faith, Father, I pray, help me to only focus on the good qualities my wife displays, and to compliment her each and every day.

Father, I pray that You will help me to experience the same hurts and pains my wife encounters and Father, build my compassion for her, so I will be able to comfort her in the way she needs me.

Father, last, but surely not the least, Lord make me to always consider my wife truly as a gift from You and that I was made for her.

In Jesus' Name I pray,

Amen

FOR MARRIED (WOMAN)

Father, during creation, as You completed each day's assignment, You said, "It was good." But when You saw that man was all alone, You said, "It is not good for the man to be alone." "I will make him a helper who is of himself."

Father, You took the rib along with all the female organs out of the man and formed a woman and brought her to the man, so that one half would complete the other half again.

Father, You called one half man and my half woman. Father, help me realize that I was taken from man, and that I am bone of his bone, and flesh of his flesh. Father, because of You, he calls me his wife for I was taken from him. Father, help me be able to leave my father and mother and bond with my own husband because now our two halves have become one flesh, one soul, and one spirit again. Lord help me bond with the Mighty Man of Valor You sent me.

Father, my question is, "How can I find a Mighty Man of Valor?" unless he comes from You, for his price is far above precious stones. Father, I thank You for blessing me with a Mighty Man of Valor. Lord help me to love my husband the same way Christ loves me.

Father, Your Word says that I am to submit to my own Mighty Man of Valor, and I will obtain favor from You. Father, I pray that You will help me to love honor and submit to my own husband's leadership in our home in the same manor as the Lord Jesus Christ submits to You.

Father, I pray that as I follow the entire teachings of Your Word, You will bless my family with a double dose of Your favor.

Father, I pray that You will help me fulfill my marital duty to my husband. Lord help me realize that I do not have authority over my own body and that my husband does. Equally, help my husband realize that he does not have authority over his own body but I do. Lord help us to not deprive one another - except when we agree, for a time, to devote ourselves to prayer. Lord, I pray that You will help us to be of one mind and Spirit.

Father, I pray that You will show me how to love You with all my heart, with my entire mind, and with all my strength and to love my husband as Jesus loves me. Father, help me to follow Your Word completely, and to except the bitter parts of Your Word, as I accept the sweet parts.

Father, show me how to be strong and to remain on the wall that You and I are building in my marriage.

Father, if a time should come that my husband may be struggling in his faith, Father, help me to only focus on the good qualities my husband displays, and to compliment him each and every day.

Father, I pray that You will help me to experience the hurts and pains my husband encounters and Father, build my compassion for him, so I will be able to comfort him in the way he needs me. Father, last but surely not the least, Lord make me to always consider myself truly as a gift to my husband and him a gift to me, from You.

In Jesus' Name I pray,

Amen

FOR DISAPPOINTMENT

Father, I am in a state of defeat, I pray for You to help me to bear life's disappointments. My high hopes has all but departed from me. Father, I pray that You will help me turn from my evil thoughts, and bitterness that hold me captive. Father, teach me how to hear Your voice and pay attention to Your wisdom.

Father, I pray to You, Lord that You won't let life's terrible disappointments overtake me. Father, help me to realize that the result of my expressing my disappointments to others is like spreading bitter poison. Lord Jesus, help me to live in peace with all of life's disappointment.

Father, help me, to choose to live a clean and Holy life, so when I am in the presence of those who do not know You, they will see that Your Son, the Lord Jesus Christ, lives in me. Lord Jesus, You know what is best for me, help me to see that even this bitter disappointment I am going through may not be as bad as it seems.

Father, Your Word teaches that all things work together for good to us that love You, to we who are the called according to Your purpose.

Father, please change my heart and give me a new heart, one that is capable of allowing the Holy Spirit to make intercession for me, according to Your will, for I know not what to pray like I should.

Father, help me not to blame others unjustly, nor be too hard on myself for life's disappointments.

Holy Spirit, encourage me in my suffering that it is God who makes "all things - even my sorrows, my trials and all persecutions - work together in my life for my good."

I praise You Lord for the eye and strength of my God is upon me, so nothing can cause me to cease from praying and believing, till the day of the Lord. Father, I raise You, for now I am standing fast in liberty, because Christ has made me free, for the yoke of bondage has been lifted.

In Jesus' Name I pray,

Amen

FOR NIGHTLY PROTECTION

Father, as You lay me down to sleep, I pray to You Lord my soul to keep, Father, I give You praises for watching over me today. Father, You protected and provided for my family and me throughout this entire day.

Father, I lift our family banner in Your presence so that You will send Your angels to camp around my home and provide protection throughout the night during this time of rest for my family and me. Lord, I pray that You were pleased with my family and me for our service to You today.

Father, I pray that You will bring us safely into tomorrow. Father, I pray that Your angels will look over my family and me, so that the evil one will not steal anything from us the whole time we are asleep.

Father, I know we will rest in peace because You will be with us throughout the night. In fact, You will be like a wall of protection surrounding us as we sleep.

Father, these are the Words I sing to You, at the end of each and every day. "The Lord is my rock, my fortress, and my Savior. The Lord is my rock, in which I find protection, the Lord is my shield and the strength of my salvation, and so whom shall I fear."

The Lord is my stronghold, my high tower, and my Savior. Yes, Lord, You are the One who saves my family and me even while we are sleeping. I will sing praise to You, Lord, because You are worthy to be praised. I will sing praises to You, Lord, because we find protection in You, not only today, but each and every day.

I give praises to You Lord for not only are You worthy of praise, but because we came to You for protection today. Lord, You did not let us be put to shame before our enemies, because our enemies could not reach me.

Father, the honor of Your name, led me out of their danger. Lord I sing praises to You today, because You always do what is right. Your promises always prove to be true.

Father, Your goodness was so great today, You have stored up great blessings and favor in heaven for me and my family, who honor You. Father, You have done so much for us today, that the whole world is watching us.

Father, thank You for forgiving my sins and granting us peace and quietness through out the coming night so my family and I may serve You even better tomorrow.

Father, I know my family and I will rest in peace tonight, because the eye and strength of our God is upon us, so nothing can cause us to cease from praying and believing.

Father, I praise You, for now we are standing fast in liberty, because Christ has made me free.

In Jesus' Name I pray,

Amen

FOR GOD'S POWER

Father, at times it's very hard for me to truly serve You, because I have no power of myself. Lord, I pray for Your power, so it will help me to choose this day and everyday to serve You and not the gods which my fathers served, that were on the other side of my wilderness which You brought me through, and truly not the gods of the pleasures of the lust of my flesh.

Father, I pray that You will bring my household and me into a place where we will serve only You. Father, I pray, in Jesus' name, that You will fill my heart with Your love, so I can love You more than I love myself. Father, help me to wait patiently for You to empower me in Your strength. Then I will be brave and courageous. And Father, make me to wait patiently in Your presence for You to fill me with trustworthiness, so I can serve You better.

Father, I bring all my cares, troubles, fears and disappointments to You, because I recognize You as my loving and most merciful Savior. Lord, I give You all praises for making me a new person. I am not the same anymore, for the old life is gone. A new life has begun.

Father, thank You for taking away from me all the filth and evil that was in my life and making me humble, by giving me a new heart one that allows me to accept the good news that will save my soul.

Father, thank You for empowering me with the same mind that was in the Lord Jesus Christ, so now when I listen to Your messenger I will understand and obey. Father, I know that if I do not obey, I am only fooling myself. For if I just listen to Your Word, and do not obey it, it is like looking at my face in a mirror but doing nothing to improve my appearance, and even forgetting what I even look like.

Father, I realize that I will never be able to earn Your approval by trying to keep Your laws within myself. So, make me die to the law by crucifying me with Christ, so that I might live my life in Christ. Father, I thank You for sending Your Son, who loved me and gave His life for me. Now, I myself no longer live but Christ lives in me, and through me.

Father, help me be able to always seek first Your kingdom, and all Your righteousness, so that You will add all good things to me. And Father, I claim Your promise that nothing can ever separate me from Your love - not death, life, the angels, demons, my fears or my worries.

Not even the powers of Hell can keep me away from Your love. Even if I soar high above the sky or fall to the depths of the ocean, nothing in all creation will ever be able to separate me from Your love that comes to me through the blood of Christ Jesus my Lord.

In Jesus' Name I pray,

Amen

FOR POWER TO NOT GOSSIP

Father, Your Word says that I must not go about spreading slander among Your people, and that I must not jeopardize my neighbor's life.

And that I must not sit around and slander a brother/sister, and even my own mother's son/daughter.
And that You are Lord.

Father, Your Word says that a gossip goes around revealing secrets, but those who are trustworthy can keep a confidence.
And that You are Lord.

Father, Your Word goes on to say that people accuse others falsely and send them to their death, because people are filled with idol worshipping and take part in indecent activities.
And that You are Lord.

Father, Your Word says that a faithful person will not disclose what they are trusted with, unless Your honor and the real good of society require it.

Father, I pray, help me to be a good faithful person that produces good deeds and Father, give me a good heart, because whatever is in my heart determines what I say.

Father, I pray, help me to break this evil person addiction that causes me to be a habitual Hypocrite, and makes me sit around and slander others.

Father, I pray, help me to serve You whether people honor me or despise me, whether they slander me or Praise me.

Lord I pray, give me strength to resist slandering others, even when they lay traps for me, or make plans to ruin me.

Lord help me to be deaf to all their threats, help me to be silent before them as one who cannot speak, and choose to hear nothing, and make no reply.

Father, help me to be kind to others, tenderhearted, forgiving, just as You through Christ has forgiven me.

Help me to wait for You, O Lord. Because You will answer for me,

And that You are Lord.

In Jesus' Name I pray,

Amen

FOR REPENTANCE

Most merciful Father, who lives in Heaven, may Your name be honored. Father, Yours is the kingdom, and the power, and the glory, forever.

Father, You said "If I, one of Your children, who is called by Your name, if I would humble my self, and pray, and seek Your face, and turn from my wicked ways; then You would hear my cry all the way from Heaven, and would forgive my sins, and heal me.

Lord You promised that Your eyes would be open, and Your ears attended unto my prayer of repentance.

Father, If I have found favor in thy sight, O Lord and if it pleases You, let my eternal salvation is given to me at my petition, and at my request:

Hear my cry, O Lord and I will testify unto You, and I will always listen to You. And it shall come to pass, and I will diligently learn the ways of Your eternal salvation.

Then I will be able to turn from my evil way, and from my evil doings, and serve You, Lord the highest Living God, forever.

Lord You sent John the Baptist, preaching in the wilderness saying, "repent ever one for the kingdom of Heaven is at hand." So bring forth fruits worthy of repentance.

Father, I realize that I have sinned, and have fallen short of Your glorious standard. Father, I also realize that the wages of sin is death, but the free gift of God is eternal life through Christ Jesus the Lord.

Father, the Lord Jesus Christ said, "He did not come to call the righteous, but sinners to repentance." And saying, "the time is fulfilled, and the kingdom of God is at hand: repent all, and believe the Gospel."

Father, I confess with my mouth that Jesus is Lord and I believe in my heart that You raised Him from the dead. Father, I believe in my heart that by repenting, this will make me right with You.

Father, I also believe by confessing with my mouth as the Scriptures tell me, I will not be disappointed. Father, in Jesus name take me back. This time I will study to show myself approved by You.

In Jesus' Name I pray,

Amen

FOR THE REVELATION OF JESUS CHRIST

I pray that the God of my Lord and Savior Jesus Christ, the Father of glory, will give unto me the Spirit of wisdom and revelation in the knowledge of Christ Jesus.

I pray that my eyes and my understanding will be enlightened, so I may Know what is the hope of Your calling for me and what the riches of the glory of Your inheritance is, in me.

And what is the exceeding greatness of Your power is to me, who believe, according to the working of Your mighty power in me.

Father, it is the same power, which You bestowed in Christ, when You raised Him from the dead, and set Him at Your right hand in Heavenly Places. Far above all principality, and power, and might, and dominion, and every name that is named, not only in this world, but also in that which is to come; Father, You have put all things under His feet, and gave Him to be the head over all things to the church, which is His body, the fullness of Him that fills all in all.

In Jesus' Name I pray,

Amen

FORSAKE ME NOT, O LORD

O Lord You know what I long for, O Lord You hear my every sigh. My heart beats wildly, my strength fails. Meanwhile, my enemies lay traps for me; they make plans to ruin me. They think up treacherous deeds all day long.

Father, help me to be deaf to all their threats. Help me to be silent before them as one who cannot speak. Help me choose to hear nothing they say, and help me not to reply. Help me to wait for You, O Lord.

Answer me, O Lord, my Father, I pray, "Don't let my enemies gloat over me or rejoice at my downfall." Father, I am on the verge of collapse, as I face constant pain.

My enemies are many; they hate me even though I have done nothing against them. They repay me with evil for good and oppose me because now I stand for what is right. Do not abandon me O Lord.

Father, I confess my sins. I am deeply sorry for what I have done. Do not stand at a distance, my Lord. Come quickly to help me, O Lord my Savior.

Father, I praise You, for now I am standing fast in liberty, because Christ has made me free, and I am no longer entangled in the yoke of bondage. In Jesus' Name I pray, Amen

FOR SALVATION

Father, I realize that the need for salvation goes back to man's removal from the Garden of Eden. After man sinned his life became marked by strife and difficulty.

Father, I pray that You deliver me from the power of sin, which has increasingly allowed corruption and violence to dominated my life.

Father, when You destroyed the world with the flood, You also performed the first act of salvation by saving Noah and his family. The salvation of Noah and his family was viewed by the apostle Peter as a pattern of Your full salvation, which I have received in Christ.

Lord, Your Word says, that if I believe in Jesus Christ, that I will be saved along with my entire household. Father, my prayer to You is, help me to bring Jesus into my heart and my entire household.

Father, help me to live my life right before it's too late, for time is running out. Father, help me to wake up, for the coming of my salvation is hear.

Father, I confess that I have sinned and have come short of Your glory. Father, I confess to the knowledge that the wages of my sins is death; and that Your gift to me is eternal life in Christ Jesus.

Father, by Your grace I pray, save me through my confession of faith and works, not my own faith and not by my own works, lest I should think I earned anything but as a free gift from You, for the working of Your Holy Spirit in me.

Father, I confess with my mouth that Jesus is Lord and I believe in my heart that You raised Him from the dead. Father, because of this confession, Your Word says that I am saved. Now, Holy Spirit, keep me.

In Jesus' Name I pray,

Amen

FOR SEEKING GOD FIRST

My Father, who lives in heaven, Holy is Your name, let Your kingdom come, and let Your will be done on Earth, as it is in heaven.

Father, You are my shepherd, You are the one who gives me my daily bread. Lord Your Word says that if I want anything extra, that I should ask You, and You will give it to me.

Father, teach me how to know what Your will is for me, so that when I ask for something, I will ask for the right things, and You will give it to me.

Lord, Your Word says that if I do not know Your will that I should keep searching Your Word, and I will find it.

Lord, Your Word says that if I should find the door locked, that I should keep knocking and the door will be opened to me. For everyone who asks receives and the one who searches finds and to the one who knocks the door will be opened.

Father, I know that if I ask You for bread, You will not give me a stone or if I ask for a fish, You will not give me a snake. Lord, Your Word teaches that if my earthly Father who is evil knows how to give good gifts to me, how much more will my Father in heaven give good things to me when I ask Him!

Lord, Your Word teaches that You know what I need even before I ask. Therefore, Lord, I pray, help me to seek first Your kingdom and Your righteousness and all other things will be provided for me.

Father, I pray, help me to not worry about tomorrow because tomorrow will worry about itself.

Father, Yours is the kingdom, the power, and the glory, forever.

In Jesus' Name I pray,

Amen

FOR SELF-CONTROL

Father, I pray for You to help me to gain control of my mind, so I will have all of my faculties under self-control.

Father, help me in the same way to gain respect of first You, then of others. Father, even in the words I speak, help me not to speak evil of others. Father, help me to always exercise self-control and be faithful in everything I do.

Father, help me to always be involved within my surroundings and help me to always be forgiving of others and to always be under self-control, with my interest fixed on that which is good.

Father, I pray teach me how to be an example to others so they may also exercise self-control and we all will be worthy of respect, as we all live wisely. Father, with self-control I will be able to build strong faith and be filled with love and patience.

Father, with self-control I will be able to follow Your instructions and to turn my life from godless living and sinful pleasures. Father, help me realize that it is impossible for me to live in this evil world with out self-control, right conduct, and devotion to You.

Father, help me to think clearly, so I can get to know You better because Your Word teaches that by building a closer relationship with You, it leads to better self-control.

Self-control leads to patient and endurance, and which leads to Godliness. Father, Your Word teaches that You did not give me the Spirit of fear but the Spirit of power, of love and of a sound mind, because with these I will be able to exercise self-control.

Father, I pray, teach me how to exercise patience over power, for it is better to have self-control than to conquer a city. Father, Your word says, "A person without self-control is as defenseless as a city with broken-down walls." Father, teach me self-control.

In Jesus' Name I pray,

Amen

FOR SPIRITUAL EYES

Almighty and merciful Father, I pray for You to build in me Spiritual eyes so I can see beyond my human capabilities. For it is written, eye has not seen, nor ear heard, and neither have entered into the heart of man, the things which You have prepared for us that love You.

Father, I thank You for revealing Spiritual things to me. I know the Holy Spirit searches all things, yes, even the deep things of the Lord. Father, how can I see the things of God unless the Holy Spirit opens my eyes?

Father, I pray that You blind me to the things of this world, and open wide my eyes so I will receive Spiritual sight, which is of the Lord. Father, help me to see, not in the sight which man's wisdom reveals, but the things Your Holy Spirit reveals, comparing Spiritual things with the Spiritual.

Father, I realize that the natural man receives not the things of the Spirit of the Lord because they are foolishness unto him. Neither can he know them, because they are Spiritually discerned. Father, I pray that You will give me Spiritual eyes, and Spiritual discernment, so I will be able to judge all things. But let not the world judge me.

Father, who can see through Your eyes, but we that are borne of Christ and sit with Jesus in the throne room of the Lord.

Almighty and merciful Father, I pray that You grant that my sight will not be bound by what my eyes can see. Give me the grace of Your vision to understand Spiritual things. Glorious Father, in Jesus Christ's name I pray, give me Spiritual eyes to see those things which are not as though they were.

Father, I give You praises, because the reason I can see Spiritual things, is because You have revealed them to me through Your eyes. Father, the Holy Spirit searches out everything and shows me, even Your deep secrets.

Father, thank You for flooding my heart with Spiritual discernment, now my eyes can see the wonderful future You have promised me.

In Jesus' Name I pray,

Amen

SPIRITUAL WARFARE

Father, Your Word says, "That the hour will come, and has come when the true worshipers shall worship You in Spirit and in Truth for You seek such to worship You."

Father, I realize that You are a Spirit, and the Truth, and if I am to worship You, I must worship You in Spirit and in Truth. Lord I pray that You will teach me how to worship You in Spirit and in Truth. Father, help me to understand that the battles I fight now that I am a Christian are not fought in the natural but in the unseen. Lord teach me how to be a Supernatural fighter.

Father, I pray that You will reveal to me by Your Spirit what Paul meant when he said, "That the battles I fight are not against people, but against the rulers, against the authorities, against the world powers of darkness, and against the spiritual forces of evil in high places.

Father, Your Word points out that spiritual wars are wars that You declare, lead and win. Father, these wars began when sin entered into the world. Lord, You declared hostility between the seed of woman and the seed of the devil as he entered into the serpent way back in the Garden of Eden. Father, teach me how to recognize and fight.

Father, I pray for You to teach me how to fight spiritual wars against the rulers, against the authorities, against the world powers of this darkness and against the spiritual forces of evil in the heavens.

Father, I realize that the concept of spiritual warfare is that since You declare the war and I should consider myself consecrated to You.

Father, Paul said, "That I must be strengthened by Your, vigorous energy and strength. Father, I pray that You show me how to put on all the Spiritual Armor that You have made available for all believers.

Father, I pray for You to show me how to take up Your full Spiritual Armor and make me able to not only resist evil, but to make a stand in these evil days, by showing me how to prepare everything, so I can make my stands.

Father, loose the fruit of the Spirit Longsuffering, and I will stand even more. Father, teach me how to stand with the belt of Truth around my waist. Father, teach me how to put the armor of Righteousness on my chest, and teach me how to get my feet sandaled with the readiness of the Gospel of Peace.

Father, in every situation, teach me how to take the Shield of Faith, because with it I will be able to extinguish the flaming arrows of the evil one. Father, teach me how to take the Helmet of Salvation, along with the Sword of the Spirit, which is Your Word.

Father, with every prayer and request, teach me how to pray at all times in the Spirit and stay alert with all perseverance, as I make intercession for all the saints.

Father, ask Jesus to enter into intercession also for me, that the message may be given to me when I open my mouth to make known with boldness the mystery of Your Gospel. For this I am an ambassador of Jesus Christ. Father, I pray that I will be bold enough in Your might to speak, as I should.

Father, You did not give me a Spirit of fear, but of power, of love and of a sound mind. For the weapons of my warfare are not carnal but mighty through You, Lord, for the pulling down of strongholds.

Father, I praise You for You have placed a hedge of protection around me and no weapon that the enemy has can prosper.

In Jesus' Name I pray,

Amen

THE LORD IS MY SHEPHERD II

Lord You are my Shepherd. You supply me with whatever I need, therefore, I want for nothing, I and if I do not have everything I desire, teach me to understand that it is either not fit for me, not good for me or I shall have it in due time.

Father, You have given me support and the comfort of a good life. Your good hands supplies me with my daily bread. Father, the greatest abundance to me is to taste the goodness of Your love in all my enjoyments.

Father, You arranged the green pastures, so that food is provided for me. Father, the Word of Life is the nourishment for my Spirit man. Father, it's like milk to a baby. Lord Your perfect will for me is that I lie down in Your green pastures.

Father, I pray that You will not let me think that it is enough that I just pass through the green pastures, but make me to lie down in them. Help me to endure in them, and make it my rest. Lord it is by Your grace that my soul and Spirit are fed.

Father, it is You who leads me beside the still waters. Lord as I feed on Your goodness, it is my prayer that You will help me follow Your direction, as You lead me by Your authority, Your Word, and Your Spirit.

Father, provide for me not only food and rest but also refreshments and pleasure. Father, one of the comforts and joy of living and walking in Your Spirit, is the still waters to which I am led. Lord I pray that as You lead me by the streams which flow from the fountain of living water, and teach me how to drink, I will never thirst again.

Father, I praise You, because You do not lead me to standing waters that are corrupt and filthy, not to the troubled sea, or to the rapid rolling floods, but to the silent swirling waters. Father, these are the running waters, which agree with my Spirit as it silently flows toward You.

Father, help me to submit totally to You as You lead me in the paths of righteousness. Lord help me to be led in the way of righteousness, for it is the way of my duty. Father, I pray that You instruct me by Your Word and direct me by Your power, principles, Your divine guidance, and Your care.

Father, these are the paths in which all believers desire to be led and kept. Father, help me never to turn to the side or off the path. Lord as You lead me beside the still waters, comfort me, and teach me then I will always walk in the paths of righteousness. Father, I realize that it is the works of righteousness that brings me peace. Father, I realize that I cannot walk the path unless You lead me.

Father, restore my soul if I go astray. Lord like a lost sheep, I may sometime miss the way and turn to the side onto other paths. Father, if I do, my prayer is, that You show me my error and lead me into true repentance and bring me back to my duty again.

Lord, I pray that You will always restore my soul, by sending the Holy Spirit to correct me. Lord though You may suffer me to fall into sin, I know You will is not to suffer me to lie still in it. Father, You recover me when I am sick, revive me when I am faint and restore my soul when it departs me.

Father, You shall always be my strong tower, because You always assure me that You are the one who leads me, feeds me, and will not leave me hanging in danger.

Even, though I walk through the valley of the shadow of death, I will fear no evil, because You are always with me. Father, even though death is the king of terrors, it brings no fear to the sheep of God, because the Lord Jesus Christ's death on the cross defeated death.

Father, I thank You for washing me in the blood of the Lamb of God. Now I no more tremble at death. O death where is your sting? Father, I praise You because You have taken the evil fear out of death for the children of God and now death cannot separate me from Your love. Therefore, death can do me no real harm, it can only kill my body, but it cannot touch my soul. Father, I thank You for Your gracious presence in my life.

Father, You are always with me. Your Word and Spirit always comforts me. Father, You are my rod and my staff. I pray that You will always comfort me, even when it is time for me to die. Father, I know that out of body is present with You, Lord. Father, it is the rod of Christ that strengthens and comforts me.

Father, You prepare a table before me in the presence of my enemies. Father, You make it possible for me to feast in spite of my enemies, for You give me the confidence that Your favor will forever attend me. Father, You anoint my head with oil, You fill my cup until it runs over. Father, even though my enemies seek to destroy me, You deliver me and deal most liberally with me in spite of them.

Father, this beautiful Psalm most admirably sets before me, this revelation. "The Lord Is my Shepherd," who rules over and feeds me. Surely goodness and mercy shall follow me all the days of my life and I will dwell in the house of the Lord forever.

In Jesus' Name I pray,

Amen

FOR THE ABILITY TO LOVE

Father, You set the standards of what love is, by loving the world so much, that You gave Your only begotten Son along with this promise, that "Who ever will believe in the person of the Lord Jesus Christ will not perish, but have everlasting life."

Father, You are the One who gives me the ability to love. Lord help me to love You with my entire mind, with all my entire heart, with all my soul and with all my strength, for this is the greatest commandment.

Father, help me to love my neighbors as Jesus loves me, for there is no greater love that a person can do than to lay down their life for their brother/sister. Father, teach me how to plead in intercession prayer for others.

Father, although I speak in languages of heaven and earth, my prayer is, teach me how to love You, because without love, I would only be making meaningless noise like a loud gong or a clanging cymbal.

Father, although You give the gift of prophecy and knowledge of the future, Lord bless me also with the ability to love others, for without the ability to love others what good would I be?

Father, thank You for the gift of faith, now I can speak to a mountain and it will move out of my way

Lord, I pray for a new heart to house the new Spirit, You have put inside of me. Father, I pray for You to take the stony heart out of me and give me a Spirit-filled heart, one capable of loving You first, then all others.

Father, with a new heart filled with Your Spirit, I will be able to walk in Your statutes, and keep Your judgments, when it comes to loving others. Father, help me to be able to always walk in the light of love.

Father, I know that love is only one of Your attributes; it is also an essential part of Your Nature. "God is love," Father, You are the personification of perfect love. Father, Your love surpasses all my powers of understanding. Love like this is everlasting, free, and sacrificial, that endures to the end.

Father, I pray, help me to always remember that love is patient and kind. Love is not jealous, boastful, proud, or rude. Father, help me realize that love does not demand its own way and that love is not irritable and it keeps no record of when it has been wronged.

Father, help me to realize that love is never glad about injustice but rejoices whenever the truth wins out. Love never gives up, Love never loses faith, Love is always hopeful, and Love endures through every circumstance. Love will last forever.

Father, I pray forever increasing faith in You, and for the ability to speak knowledgeably, with Your wisdom. Father, I pray without ceasing for Your love to compel me to participate in the work of Your kindness, as I intercede in love for others always.

In Jesus' Name I pray,

Amen

FOR THE BAPTISM OF THE HOLY SPIRIT

Lord You are my Father who lives in heaven, Holy is Your name. Lord let Your kingdom come; let Your will be done in me, as it is written in heaven.

Blessed are You, Lord, the Father of my Lord and Savior Jesus Christ. Thank You, heavenly Father, for blessing me with Your Spiritual blessings.

Father, Your Word says that You chose me before the foundation of the world, that I should be holy. Father, You predestined me to be one of the adopted children through Jesus Christ Himself, according to the good pleasures of Your will, to the praise of the glory of Your grace, wherein You have made me accepted in Your heavenly family.

Father, I have redemption through the blood of Jesus, and forgiveness of my sins, according to the riches of Your grace. Father, my prayer is to be made complete in Jesus Christ, who is the head over all principalities and powers.

Father, Your Word says, Jesus stood and cried, saying, If I thirst for righteousness, that I should come unto Him, and drink. And that He would baptize me with the Holy Ghost, and with fire:

Father, Your Word says, that my believing in Jesus, as the Holy Scripture says, out of my belly will flow rivers of living water. And Jesus also said, that I will receive power, after the Holy Ghost comes upon me: and I shall be Witnesses unto Him both in my home, and in all the world,
and in the uttermost part of the Earth. Father, like on the day of Pentecost when the believers were all filled with the Holy Ghost, and began to speak with other tongues, as the Spirit gave them utterance. Lord my prayer is fill me with the Holy Ghost.

Father, I remember the words of the Lord how that He said, John indeed baptized with water; but He will baptize and fill me with the Holy Ghost and with fire.

Lord, my prayer is, fill me with the Holy Ghost and with fire. Father, with the Baptism of the Holy Spirit comes new manifestation and new power. It is the Spiritual relation to Christ Father, Jesus said, that these signs shall follow me if I believe; that in His name I will cast out devils; I will speak with new tongues. If I take up serpents; and if I drink any deadly thing, it shall not hurt me, and that I can lay hands on the sick, and they will recover. Lord, baptize me in the power of Your Holy Spirit. Father, Yours is the kingdom, and the power, and the glory, forever. In Jesus' Name I pray, Amen.

FOR THE FRUITS OF THE SPIRIT

Father, I praise You for blessing me with the fruits of Your Holy Spirit. I will be very careful to observe all the commandments which You commanded me, as I walk in all Your ways and hold fast to my service to You, with all my heart, with all my soul, with all my strength and with my entire mind. Father, I thank You for giving me the ability to walk in the fruits of Your Holy Spirit.

Love - Father with Your kind of love, I will be able to love my neighbor in the same way You have loved me. Father, build my faith so I can activate the fruit of the Spirit - love, which is born of You, as I am born of You. Father, thank you for the gift of fruit of the Spirit - love.

Joy - because You have put gladness in my heart. Father, Jesus was filled with the joy of the Holy Spirit. Father, show me how to loose the fruit of the Spirit - joy and laughter and Father help me to leap for the fruit of Spirit - joy.

Peace - because You are the God of all my peace. Father, I pray that You will teach me how to live life in Your peace and to rejoice and be complete. Lord, comfort me, so that my mind will always rest in the knowledge that the fruit of the Spirit - peace, is already in me.

Longsuffering - because in everything as Your child, I commend myself by great endurance, by afflictions, by hardship, by pressures, by beatings, by imprisonments, by riots, by labors, by sleepless nights, by times of hunger, by purity, by knowledge, by patience, and by kindness. Father, help me to activate the fruit of the Spirit - longsuffering.

Kindness - because it's an attribute of Yours, Lord a quality desirable but not consistently found in humans. Father, I pray that You will help me to understand divine kindness and how to be consistently kind to others. Father, the fruit of the Spirit - kindness is manifest in the full salvation that comes through the Lord Jesus Christ.

Goodness - because Your goodness is the solid rock to the truth of scripture. Your goodness is praised in the Psalms. Jesus affirms Your goodness when speaking about the Father. Peter echoes the language the Psalmist said "Taste and see that the Lord is good!" Father, I pray, help me to be a faithful follower, and bless me with the fruit of the Spirit - goodness.

Faithfulness - Father, in the Old Testament, Your faithfulness and covenant love are closely related. David and other godly people chose to walk the faithful way - the way of truth.

Father, I pray that You will help me to always believe in You and to exhibit true faithfulness and steadfast love towards You and others.

Gentleness - Father, You are the supreme example of gentleness. Lord You care tenderly for me, as You gently lead me by Your Spirit. Father, help me to be gentle and humble in heart and help me to follow Jesus' example, and to treat people gently.

Meekness - Father, Your majesty rides on victoriously, for the cause of truth, righteousness, and meekness. Lord I pray, teach me humility like You did Paul. He was oppressed and afflicted; yet he did not open his mouth. Like a lamb that is led to slaughter, like a sheep that is silent before its shears. Father, show me how to operate in the fruit of the Spirit – meekness - and help me not to open my mouth.

Temperance - Father, You set the terms for being patient, therefore I pray for patience and moderation when dealing with others.

Father, beside these, give me diligence and add to my faith virtue; and to virtue knowledge; and to knowledge temperance; and to temperance patience; and to patience godliness; and to godliness brotherly kindness; and to brotherly kindness charity and endurance. For if these things be in me and abound they will make me. I will neither be barren or unfruitful in the knowledge of my Lord Jesus Christ.

Self-control - Father, Your Word teaches that a double-minded believer is unstable in all their ways. Lord I pray that You will help me to control all of my emotions, desires, and action, by my own will.

Father, don't let me think myself more than I am. When self-control is what I need, Lord, help me to exercise Christian knowledge and discernment concerning Your will.

Let there be the practical fruit of the Spirit of the self-control over the lusts of my flesh. Father, I pray for self-control that will move weakness and impart strength, patient, and endurance as I endure in Your godliness. Father, I pray You will continue to bless me with these fruits of Your Spirit; Love, Joy, **Peace, Longsuffering, Kindness, Goodness, Faithfulness, Gentleness, Meekness, and Self-control.**

I pray daily and I crucify my flesh daily from the affections and lusts as I live in Your Spirit, I will also walk in Your Spirit.

In Jesus' Name I pray,

Amen

THE LORD'S PRAYER

My Father, who lives in heaven, teach me to pray like Jesus instructed His disciples. Lord, I know that I do not have to pray in the very words Jesus prayed, but "after His manner."

Lord, teach me how not to pray by using vain repetitions. Lord help me to pray the words that will help me develop a very tender relationship between You and me. Lord, help me to be able to speak to You, like a child speaks to their father.

Lord, help me to develop my heart so that I will recognize You as the Lord of the Bible. Lord, help me to be secure and to pray with boldness when I come before You.

Lord, help me to pray for longer periods of time that I may be heard by You. Lord, teach me to seek those things, which are above. Lord I pray that You will also teach me that this earth, in which I live, is not my native country, but that heaven is my home, because It is where You live.

Lord, I pray, help me to always honor Your name, Lord, help me to magnify Your great name in my heart and to sanctify it in all the earth, which You created according to Your will and purpose.

Lord, help me to sanctify Your name, as the angels sanctify You in the highest Heaven. Lord, I know that as I sanctify Your name, it does not make You Holy; it is for me to acknowledge and declare that You are Holy. Lord, I magnify and glorify Your name for all of Your perfections. Lord, You are sanctified within Yourself.

Lord, I pray, implant Your grace and Holiness in my heart, as well as the hearts of all Your people. Lord, restore the purity of Your worship by pouring out Your Holy Spirit in the world.

Lord, let Your kingdom come soon, in its fullness and in its final triumph over evil. Lord, not my will, but Your will be done here in the Earth, just as it is in Heaven. Lord, I pray that You will give me my food for today, not for the future, but for today.

Lord, forgive my sins and my shortcomings, and help me forgive those who have sinned against me, and measure me as I measure others. Lord, I know that You cannot forgive the sins I commit against others if I am unforgiving. Father, help me to realize that Your kind of forgiveness must be a completed act on my part, even before I can to pray to You.

Lord, forgiveness is difficult at times, but I know that it is essential. Lord help me to forgive others by sending the Holy Spirit to always be present when I pray.

Lord, help me to get the victory over my flesh, and Lord, help me to always make an earnest effort on my part to not yield to temptation. Lord shield me from it. Father, thank You for not allowing me to be tempted beyond what I am able to resist, by always providing a way for me to escape it, and Lord able me to endure to the end.

Lord, when I enter into temptation, help me come out victorious by turning it into a blessing instead of a curse. Lord, I pray that I will receive the crown of life, which You have promised to those who love You and keep Your Word.

Lord, deliver me from the evil one; also deliver me from the evil thoughts in my own heart.

Father, Yours is the kingdom, and the power, and the glory, forever.

In Jesus' Name I pray,

Amen

MAGNIFICENT IS THE NAME OF THE LORD

O Lord, my Lord, how magnificent is Your name throughout the Earth! Father, You have covered the heavens with Your majesty.

Father, because of Your adversaries, You have established a stronghold for the mouths of children and nursing infants, to silence the enemy and the avenger.

Father, as I observe Your heavens, the work of Your fingers, the moon and the stars which You set in place, I think, what am I that You remember me, a son of man. Yet, You look after me.

Father, You put everything under Your feet - all the sheep and oxen, as well as animals in the wild, birds of the sky and fish of the seas.

O Lord, my Lord, how magnificent is Your name throughout the Earth!
In Jesus' Name I pray,
Amen

FOR THE POWER TO PRAY

My Father, who lives in heaven, Holy is Your name. Father, I lift Your name on high, I give You praises, and I also come to glorify Your name, and give You thanks when I pray to You. Father, I give You all praise, glory, and honor, because my ability to pray comes from You. For You have given me the power to pray. Father, You are omniscient, omnipresent, and omnipotent.

Father, You know my heart, You also know that without the Holy Spirit, it is impossible for me to pray. Father, I pray that You send Your Holy Spirit so that He will teach me how to pray, as well as plead for me, so I can be in harmony and within Your perfect will when I pray to You in Jesus' name.

Father, I know that You cause everything to work together for my good when I pray, because Father, I know that You love me.

Father, You know my heart, for You have chosen me to become one of Your sons/daughters. Lord, You sent Jesus, Your only begotten Son to the Earth, to be the firstborn of new breed, and You have given Him many brothers and sisters. Thank You, Father, for making me one of Your sons/daughters.

Thank Lord for choosing me. You called me, to come to You, and You gave me the right to stand with You, and be a part of Your holy family.

Father, it's because of Your sending the Holy Spirit to me, that I am able to petition You for the power to pray. Father, I know that I have no power within myself. I also know that I myself am not worthy to petition You in prayer. Therefore, I humble myself before You. Lord, teach me to pray.

Father, You make me study Your Word, and I thank You for giving me Your wisdom and understanding. Father, thank You for granting me Your power and strength. Now I have might the ability, to produce mighty works for You.

Lord Jesus, You command me, to "build my faith in You" so that You will give me power when I pray. Lord, You said, "Verily, I say unto you, that anytime I tell any mountain, be removed, and be cast into the sea, and shall have not doubt in my heart, but believe those things which I said, it shall come to pass, and I will have anything I pray for.

Father, I pray for You to teach me how to walk in Your power, and unlimited faith, then when I pray, nothing will be impossible for me, and all my prayers, will be answered.

Father, Your Word teaches, "the effectual fervent prayer of a righteous servant availed much." Lord teach me, through the power of prayer how to always be righteous. Father, make me a righteous servant and open up the heavens and send me Your fruits when I pray.

Father, I give You praise and glory. Father, I worship You. Lord, I lift Your name on high.

In Jesus' Name I pray,

Amen

FOR TRUSTING IN GOD

Father, You are my rock; in You will I trust. You are my shield and the horn of my salvation, my high tower, and my refuge. You are my Savior.

Father, Your way is perfect. Your Word is tried. You are my buckle, and in You will I trust.

Father, whenever I am in battle, I cry out to You, Lord, in hopes to entreat You, because, in You do I put my trust.

Father, in You do I put my trust, because You save me from all who persecute me, You deliver me.

Father, in You, I put my trust, and I will not be afraid of what man can do to me. Preserve me, Lord, for in You do I put my trust.

Lord, You are my strength. In You, I put my trust. Lord, You are my buckle and the horn of my salvation.

Some trust in chariots, and some in horses, but I will remember the name of the Lord, my God.

Lord, You have put a new song in my mouth, and I will sing praise unto You, Lord, and many shall see it, and repent of their sins, because in You do I put my trust.

And You, Father, will bring many down into the pit of destruction, bloody and deceitful people shall not live out half their days, but in You do I put my trust.

Lord, I will praise Your Word, I will not fear what flesh can do unto me, for in You do I put my trust.

It is good for me to draw near to You, Lord. I have put my trust in You, Lord, and I know that every Word of Yours is pure. You are a shield unto me; for in You do I put my trust.

Father, I do not put my trust in the world's riches, and I had the sentence of death in myself, so I do not trust in myself, but in You, Lord, who raise the dead.

Father, You are my rock, in You will I trust. You are my shield and the horn of my salvation, my high tower and my refuge, my Savior,

in You do I put my trust.

In Jesus' Name I pray,

Amen

FOR TRUTHFULNESS

Father, I pray that You conform me, by the works of Your Holy Spirit, so I will be as truthful as Jesus was. Lord, make me to be obedient to Your standards and customs. Lord, shape my character so that I will practice the same behavior and beliefs, as did Jesus, for He set those standards.

Lord, I know that truth is a fundamental, moral and a personal quality of Yours. Father, You are merciful, gracious, longsuffering and just. Father, You are great in goodness and truth.

Father, Your mercy, and truth are joined together with works, precepts and judgments and are done in righteousness. The psalmist declared: "Your law is truth, all Your commandments are truth and the entirety of Your Word is truth." Because of Your perfect nature and will, Lord, You cannot lie.

Jesus was the example of righteousness while on Earth. Lord, I thank You for sending Jesus, who is the Word of God that became flesh - the only begotten Son of You, Father, full of grace and truth. Everything Jesus said was true, because He told the truth as He testified of You.

Father, send Your Spirit of truth to Live in me forever, and guide me into all truth.

Father, Jesus said that I will know the truth, and the truth will make me free. Father, teach me how to put on the whole armor of God, so I will be able to stand against the wiles of the devil. Lord help me to stand, having my loins gird about with truth, and having on the breastplate of righteousness. Father, make me always tell the truth no matter what.

In Jesus' Name I pray,

Amen

FOR UNSELFISHNESS

Father, it's because of Jesus that Your love has been poured out within my heart through the Holy Spirit whom You sent to me.

Father, I thank You for having feelings and affection for me, and for always giving of Yourself. I declare Your love as strongly as I believe in Your existence. For love is Your highest characteristic.

Father, I realize that after His baptism, as the Lord Jesus Christ came up out of the water, the Heavens were opened, and He saw Your Holy Spirit descending like a dove and settling on Him. And Your voice from Heaven said, "This is my beloved Son, and I am fully pleased with Him."

Father, I thank You for loving me even as You loved Jesus. I pray You will send Your Holy Spirit so I may remain in Your love as I obey You, just as Jesus obeyed You and remained in Your love. I pray, that You will fill me with Your joy. Father, I pray, that Your joy will overflow in me! Then I will be able to love others in the same way that You love me.

Father, in Jesus' name I praise You for sending the Lord Jesus Christ, who showed me the perfect example of how to love others. And I pray that You free me from the harmful selfish thoughts that I have towards others.

Father, free me from selfish words and deeds, and teach me how to develop a devoted heart that will bless others. Take selfishness out of my heart and replace it with the love that Jesus showed.

Father, help me to find pleasure in giving myself to the services set before me. Lord help me to find Joy in serving without thoughts of a return. Father, keep the thought of Your unselfish love always before me.

Father, I praise You, for now I am standing fast in liberty, because Christ has made me free, and I am no longer entangled in the yoke of bondage.

In Jesus' Name I pray,

Amen

WHEN I AM WEAK HE IS STRONG

Father, You are full of all glory, though I would desire to glory, I shall not be a fool; for I will say the truth but now I forbear, lest anyone should think of me above that which they see me to be or that they hear of me to be.

Father, lest I should be exalted above measure through the abundance of the revelations You show me, You have allowed me to be given a thorn in the flesh, the messenger of Satan to buffet me, lest I should be exalted above measure.

Father, I continue to ask You to make it depart from me, but You continue to show me, that Your grace is sufficient for me, and Your strength is made perfect in my weakness.

Father, I would most gladly, therefore, rather glory in my infirmities, so the power of Christ may rest upon me. Father, therefore, I take pleasure in my infirmities, in reproaches, in necessities, in persecutions and in distresses for my Lord And Savior, Jesus Christ, because when I am weak, then You are strong in me.

Father, I thank You for allowing me to experience things worthy of boasting about, but I am not going to do it. I am going to boast only about my weaknesses. For when I am weak, then You are strong.

Father, now I am glad to boast about my weaknesses, so that the power of Christ may work through me.

Father, since I know it is all for Your good, I am quite content with my weaknesses. For when I am weak, then You are strong in me, because I look to the Lord for my strength.

In Jesus' Name I pray,

Amen

WHEN I FALL DOWN

Father, I pray that You will help me build my house with Your wisdom, and to become strong in Your might, through good sense and through knowledge of Your Word. Father, show me how to fill my temple with all of Your precious riches and valuables.

Father, Your Word points out that if I am a good servant, full of Your wisdom and knowledge, that I will be mightier than a strong person.

Father, I realize, if I should fall when under pressure, it's because my wisdom and knowledge is not very mighty by its self.

Father, Your Word teaches that even though a righteous person falls seven times, they will get back up again. But that a wicked person will keep stumbling until they fall into ruin. Lord, if I fall, help me to be a righteous person that who can't stay down. Help me get back up again.

Father, Your Word teaches that if I have enough faith to get back up after I fall, I will be a righteous person, even though people in the church won't understand.

Father, I pray that You will show me how to be a righteous person as You build me in Your power and Your strength, and I will not fall. Lord, I pray, let wickedness have no place with me.

Father, help me to trust the teachings of Your Word that say, no matter how often honest people fall, You always help them to get back up again.

Father, help me not to rejoice when others, even my enemies fall into trouble. Father, don't let me be happy when they stumble. Father, Your Word teaches that You will not be pleased with me if the fall of someone else makes me happy.

Father, You are so faithful and just, Lord You have forgiven every single solitary sin I have committed. Father, You bring no condemnation. You have forgiven me. Help me forgive me. Lord, have mercy on me. If I fall down, Father, help me get back up again.

In Jesus' Name I pray,

Amen

FOR BELIEVING GOD

Father, I pray, that You will help me take courage as I trust in You, even though thing don't always turn out to my liking. Lord, I pray that You will teach me how to know that You are always with me, though different things at different times, some more difficult than others.

Father, I pray, that You will help me take courage as I trust in the knowing that You will not let me lose my life, even though the ship I am in may go down.

Father, I thank You for giving me Spiritual discernment and strength, along with the ability to know when I am hearing from You. Father, You do this because I belong to You.

Lord You stand beside me because I serve You.

Father, Your goodness has granted safety for me, every time I sail and You are in the boat. Father, because I know that You are in the boat, I can take courage, and stay in the boat, no matter how rough the waters may get.

Lord, my prayer is, help me believe it will be just as You said.

I Jesus Name I pray

Amen

FOR PRAYING GOD'S WORD

Lord, because You are personal, all of Your children can offer prayer to You. Father, as a disciple of Jesus I recognize my dependence upon You. Father, You have given me every reason to express my gratitude for the blessings You have already given me.

Lord, Your love is revealed through the marvelous incarnation life of Jesus Christ, His atoning provision at the Cross, His resurrection, as well as His continuing love that guides me through Your Holy Spirit.

Father, I know that the most meaningful prayers comes from my heart, when I place my trust in You, Lord, and the life of Jesus and His teachings of Your Word makes it possible for me to pray.

Father, You speak to me through the Bible, and I in turn, speak to You through truthful prayers, backed by the Holy Scriptures. Father, help me to develop a confident prayer life that is built on the works of Jesus Christ and His Words as shown by the prophets and apostles in the Spirit-inspired writings of the Bible.

Father, I pray, help me to be able to recognize and eliminate the sins in my life that hinder answers to my prayers, such as iniquity in my heart.

Lord, Your Word says that If I have unconfused sin in my heart, that You will not even listen to me when I pray. But I praise You, the Lord, because You do listen and pay attention to me when I pray, because when I pray, I pray Scripture and remind You of Your Word.

Lord, I praise You, because You do not ignore my prayer and do not withdraw Your unfailing love from me. Father, I declare to all people that I belong to You, Lord, that I honor You with the words of my mouth when I pray.

Lord, I pray, help me to store Your Words in my heart so I will never wander far from You, and always follow in Your paths. Father, Your Word promises and teaches that You will always answer my requests when I start doing Your works, and by helping the least of Your children.

Father, help me to pray always, as if I am away by myself with the door shut behind me, even when I am surrounded by others. Father, help me to pray to You in secret. Then You, who knows all secrets, will reward me.

Lord, when I pray, don't allow me to be like the proud Pharisee who stood by himself and prayed this prayer: "I thank You, God, that I am not a sinner like everyone else."

Lord, when I pray, help me to humble my self and be like the tax collector, who stood at a distance and dared not even to lift his eyes to heaven as he pray. Instead, he beat his chest in sorrow, saying: "O God, be merciful to me, for I am a sinner."

Lord, when I pray, help me not to come doubting or with double-mindedness, or come with a lack of faith. Father, You promised to answer my requests when I start helping the hungry and afflicted. Father, help me to remember that when I pray, to obey, and not just to listen to myself pray. If I don't obey, I am only fooling my self.

Father, the Lord Jesus Christ said to His disciples, "Have faith in You, O God." Father He assured me that I could say to any mountain, "May God lift you up and throw you into the sea," and that my command will be obeyed. All that's required is that I really believe and do not doubt in my heart.

Listen to Me! Jesus went on to say, "that I can pray for anything, and if I believe, I will have it. But when I am praying, first forgive anyone I am holding a grudge against, so that my Father in heaven will forgive my sins, too."

Father, I pray in Christ's name, help me abide in Christ and His Words, and to pray in the Spirit, obey the Lord's commandments, and ask according to Your will.

Lord, now my eyes will be open, and my ears will hear the prayer that I make in Your Son Jesus name. For You stand at my door, knocking. Lord, I pray, help me to hear Your voice, and to open the door and to let You in. Father, I pray, come in to me, and have sup with me, and me with You.

Lord, help me to understand that through prayer I can overcome the world, and that You will grant me to sit with You and Jesus around Your throne.

In Jesus' Name I pray,

Amen

PUTTING ON THE WHOLE ARMOR OF GOD

Lord, You Word commands me, be too strong in You, Lord, and in the power of Your might.

Lord, whenever I enter into Spiritual warfare, Lord, I pray, help me to always put on Your whole armor, so I will be able to stand against all the strategies of the devil.

Lord, Your Word also teaches me that my battle is not against people, but against principalities, against powers, against the rulers of the darkness of this world, and against spiritual wickedness in high places.

Therefore, I pray for You, O Lord, to help me to put on Your whole armor, Lord, so I will be able to withstand all evil, and when I have done all I can to stand, I will stand.

Lord, I will make my stand by putting on the belt of truth and the breastplate of righteousness.

And Lord, help my feet to stand on Your Word, the Gospel of Peace. And Lord, above all, I pray, help me to take the shield of faith, so that I will be able to quench all the fiery darts of the wicked.

And Lord, help me to take the helmet of salvation, and the sword of the Spirit, which is Your Word.

And last, but not least, Lord, help me to continue in prayer always with all my prayers and supplications in Your Spirit, and I will be watching with all perseverance and supplication for all saints.

In Jesus' Name I pray,

Amen

Author's Note

KEYS TO LIFE PRAYERS are not designed to teach you how to pray, but rather to show you the benefits and blessings of Praying God's Word back to Him *out loud*.

About the Author

Andrew Parker called to be a servant of God the Father and the Lord Jesus. He was called to the ministry in 1981, and has been passionately preaching and teaching ever since. He earned a master's degree in Bible Theology and took the Rhema Bible College Faith Course. He has a heart for youth and has been active in youth prison ministries. Andrew is a former counselor for youth offenders in the state of Washington Juvenile Rehabilitation system and department of corrections. He is the proud father of four sons and three daughters and grandfather of 11. He and his wife, Sieglinde, make their home is Lakewood, Wash., about 45 miles south of Seattle.

CREDITS AND ACKNOWLEDGEMENTS

First, I want to give honor and praises to God The Father, Jesus Christ, The Son, God the Holy Spirit; then I want to thank my wonderful and supportive wife, Sieglinda, my artist, Robert Jackson; my editor, Betty Anderson, and others who gave me their opinions and observations, those who prayed for me or assisted me in this project in some way, many thanks to you .The Bible versions used and Commentaries consulted in this publication include but are not limited to the King James Version (KJV), New King James (NKJV), Holman Christian Standard Bible (CSB), New Living Bible (NLB), New International Version (NIV), Revised Standard Version (RSV), The Living Bible (LB). Matthew Henry's, Barnes Notes, Adam Clarks, Jamieson-Fausset–Brown, commentaries.

For ordering copies of the Keys to Life Prayer Book or the original "Pray for Me" magnetic Prayer Board (patent pending), e-mail at **scriptureman23@comcast.net**

Appendix - Search the Scriptures

Introduction

Page 1_ - Exodus 32:11; 1 Samuel 1:15; 2 Chronicles 32:20; Psalms 73:28; Job 8:5; 1 Thess 5:17-19

Page 2 - Matt 16:19; John 17:19-22; Matt 26:39; Matt 26:42; Matt 26:44; Mark 1:35; Luke 5:16; Luke 9:29; Luke 22:32; 2 Tim 3:16

Page 4 - Matt 26:35-42; Matt 26:38; Eph 6:12-13

Page 5 - Eph 6:10-11

Page 6 - Matt 6:7

Page 7 – Genesis 1, 2; Rom 10:16,17

Page 8 - James 2:19; Matt 4:3-4,10-11

Prayers

A TIME FOR ALL THINGS
Matt 6:9; Eccl 3:1-15; John 10:10; Luke 18:29-30; Rom 13:11

AFTER GOD'S OWN HEART
Acts 13:22; 1 Sam 13:14; Prov 24:16; Gen 6:8-10; Job 9:1-13; Prov 9:8-11; 2 Sam 24:14; Rom 12:1; Philip 1:6; 2 Ch 7:14

FOR A CALEB SPIRIT
Num 13:3; Num 14:24; Gal 5:1

MIGHTY PRINCE OF VALOR
Philip 4:8-19; Judges 6:12,13; Ruth 2:1; 1 Sam 9:1; 1 Sam 16:18; 1 Kings 11:28; Job 22:8; Job 24:22; Ps 52:1; Ps 127:4; Prov 21:22; Isa 3:2; Isa 5:15; Isa 42:13; Jer 9:23; Matt 13:54; Acts 18:24; Isa 55:4; Ge 3:15; Ge 24:26; 2 Sam 23:10; 1 Ch 29:11; Isa 25:8; 1 John 5:4; Rev 15:2; Ezra 5:5; Gal 5:1; Ruth 3:11; Prov 12:4; Prov 31:10

FOR A NEW HEART
Ezek 11:19; Luke 5:37,38

FOR ACHIEVEMENT, PROSPERITY, AND SUCCESS
Ps 1:1-3; Pr 3:1-4; Pr 16:3,20; Pr 21:5; Pr 22:4; Pr 28:13,25; Ecc 10:10

FOR AN OPEN MIND
John 8:31-33; 1 Cor 7:21-24

A PRAYER FOR ANXIETY
1 Peter 5:3-8; Phil 2:28; Gal 5:1

FOR APPROACHING DEATH
2 Tim 1:10-11; Heb 2:14-15; Gal 5:1; 2 Cor 5:8

FOR AUTHORITY ON LOOSING GOD'S BLESSINGS
Eph 1:17-23; Jer 29:10-14

MIGHTY MAN OF VALOR
Philip 4:8-19; Judges 6:12,13; Ru 2:1; Isa 9:1; Isa 6:18; 1 Ki 11:28; Job 22:8; Job 24:22; Ps 52:1; Ps 127:4; Prov 21:22;
Isa 3:2; Isa 5:15; Isa 42:13; Jer 9:23; Mt13: 54; Ac 18:24;
Isa 55:4; Ge 3:15; Ge 24:26; 2 Sa 23:10; 1 Ch 29:11; Ge 24:26; 2 Sa 23:10;
1 Ch 29:11; Isa 25:8; 1 John 5:4; Re 15:2; Ezra 5:5; Gal 5:1

FOR BEING A PARENT
Mark 9:36-37; Matt 18:5; Lu 1:8-9; 2 Ti 3:15; Eph 6:4; Prov 22:6;
Matt 11:19; 2 Sam 23:6

VIRTUOUS PRINCESS
Philip 4:8-19; Judges 6:12,13; Ru 2:1; 1 Sa 9:1; 1 Sa 16:18; 1 Ki 11:28; Job 22:8; Job 24:22; Ps 52:1; Ps 127:4; Prov 21:22;
Isa 3:2; Isa 5:15; Isa 42:13; Jer 9:23; Matt 13:54; Ac 18:24;
Isa 55:4; Ge 3:15; Ge 24:26; 2 Sa 23:10; 1 Ch 29:11; Isa 25:8;
1 John 5:4; Rev 15:2; Ezra 5:5; Gal 5:1; Ruth 3:11; Prov 12:4-4, 31:10-10

VIRTUOUS WOMAN
Philip 4:8-19; Judges 6:12,13; Ruth 2:1; 1 Sam 9:1; 1 Sam 16:18; 1 Kings 11:28; Job 22:8; Job 24:22; Ps 52:1; Ps 127:4; Prov 21:22; Isa 3:2; Isa 5:15; Isa 42:13; Jer 9:23; Matt 13:54; Acts 18:24;
Isa 55:4; Ge 3:15; Ge 24:26; 2 Sam 23:10; 1 Ch 29:11; Isa 25:8; 1 John 5:4; Rev 15:2; Ezra 5:5; Gal 5:1; Ruth 3:11; Prov 12:4-4, 31:10-31

FOR CHEERFULNESS
Ps 103:1-5; Isa 53:4; Rom 8:28; 2Co 5:7; Isa 53:4

THAT CHRIST MAY LIVE IN MY HEART
Eph 3:14-21

A PRAYER FOR COMFORT
2 Cor 13:11; Gal 5:1

FOR CONVALESCENCE
3 John 2; Gal 5:1; Ezra 5:5

FOR ENDURANCE
Rom 15:1-8; 2 Cor 1:4-7; 2 Cor 6:4; Col 1:10-14; 1 Thess 1:2-3; 1 Tim 6:11-13; Titus 2:1-2; Rev 1:9; Rev 14:12

FOR FAIRNESS
Isaiah 11:1-9

PRAYER FOR FAITH
Heb 11:1, 6

FOR FORGIVENESS
Ps 130:1-4; Rom 3:23; Exodus 32:30-35; Luke 17:1-10; Acts 26:18

FOR FAITHFULNESS

Ex 3:13-15; Ps 89 and 119; Deut 7:9; Isa 49:7; Lam 3:23;
Rev 19:11, 1:5; 3:14; Heb 2:17; 3:2 and 11:6; 1 Cor 10:13;
Heb 10:23; 2 Tim 2:13; Gal 5:22; Ps 31:23; 1 John 1:9;
2 Tim 2:13; Ezra 5:5; Gal 5:1

FOR FRANKNESS
Philip 1:9-11; 1 Peter 2:1-3; Heb 5:12; Heb 5:12-13

FOR GAINING WEALTH
Deut 8:17,18; Ps 112:1-5; 2Ch 1-11; 1 Cor 10:23-33

FOR THE FULL BLESSINGS OF GOD
Eph 3:14-21

FOR WISDOM
1 King 5:12; 1 Kings 10:23,24; Exodus 31:3; 1 Kings 4: 29-34; Acts 7:22;
Prov 3:19; Prov 24:3-6; 1 Cor 12:7-11; Luke 1:75-78

FOR GRATITUDE
Rom 5:4-8; Ezra 5:5; Gal 5:1

FOR HAPPINESS
Ps 86:1-7; Ps 119:35-36; Prov 29:17-17; Eccl 2:1-11; Luke 6:20-26; Luke:27-36

FOR GAINING WEALTH
Deut 8:17-18; Ps 112:1-5; 2Chron 1:11; 1 Cor 10:23-33

OUR FAMILY PRAYER
Gen 5:1, 6:9, 10:1, 24:40, 30:30, 31:3; Josh 7:14-24:15; Ruth 3:9; Rom 12:10
Eph 3:14-21

FOR HONORING PARENTS
Ex 20:12; Lev 19:3; Deut 5:16, 21:18-21; Prov 22:6-8; Eph 6:4; Lev 19:2-3
2 Tim 2:15

FOR HOPE
Acts 2:26-27; Ezra 5:5; Gal 5:1

FOR HUMILITY
Eph 4:1-6; Col 3:12-15; Rom 12:3-6

FOR KEEPING ME TODAY
Num 6:22-27; Gen 6:8-10, 39:19-23; Exodus 33:12-23, 34:9; Num 32:5; Job 8:7; Ps 9:1-10, 30:1-5, 31:14-18, 69:13, 106:4; 2 Cor 12:9; Eph 3:7; Deut 33;
1 Cor 15:9-11
LET GO AND LET GOD
Matt 6: 5-34; Rom 12:3

FOR LIFTING UP MY FAMILY
John 12:32; Ge 42:25; Jos 9:5; 1 Ch 29:19; Ro 13:14
Matt 21:21; James 4:10

MAKING CORRECT DECISIONS

Matt 13:54; Mark 6:2; Exodus 31:1-11; James 1:5-6
1 Kings 3:5-15; Ps 111:10, 3:14; Pr 1:2

THE LORD IS MY SHEPHERD I
Ps 23: 1-24: Ps 1

FOR THE MARRIED COUPLE
Gen 2; Pr 31:10; Pr 18:22; Pr 19:4; Pr 12:4

FOR MARRIAGE (MAN)
Gen 2; Pr 31:10; Pr 18:22; Pr 19:4; Pr 12:4

FOR MARRIAGE (WOMAN)
Gen 2; Pr 31:10; Pr 18:22; Pr 19:4; Pr 12:4; 1 Cor 7:3-39; Eph 5:21

FOR DISAPPOINTMENT
Prov 5:1-4; Acts 8:22-24; Heb 12:14-16; Rom 8:28; Ezra 5:5; Gal 5:1

FOR NIGHTLY PROTECTION
Num 1:7-16; 2 Sam 22:2-51; Ps 7:1,18:30, 31:1-8, 31:19; Ezra 5:5; Gal 5:1

FOR POWER
Josh 24:15; Ps 27:14; 2 Cor 5:17; James 1:21-23; Gal 2:19-20; Matt 6:33;
Rom 8:38-39

FOR POWER TO NOT GOSSIP
Lev 19:16; Ps 50:20; Prov 11:13; Ezek 22:9; Luke 6:45; Ps 109:3; 1 Tim
5:13-14; Ps 50:20; Prov 11:9; Rev 12:10; Ps 52:4; 2 Cor 6:8; Ps 38:12-15;
Ps 34:13; 1 Peter 3:10-11; Eph 4:31-32

FOR REPENTANCE
Matt 6:9,13; 2 Chron 7:14,15; Es 7:3; Ps 81:8; Jer 12:16; Jer 23:22; Luke
5:32; Matt 3:1-2; Luke 3:8; Mark 1:15; Rom 3:23, 6:23, 10:9-11; 2 Tm 2:15

FOR THE REVELATION OF JESUS CHRIST
Eph 1:17-23

FORSAKE ME NOT, O LORD
Ps 38:1-39 Gal 5:1

FOR SALVATION
Gen 3, 6:11-13; 1 Peter 3:18-22; Rom 13:11; Titus 2:12-13; Rom 3:23, 6:23;
Eph 2:8-9; Rom 10:8-11; Ex 15:2

FOR SEEKING GOD FIRST
Matt 6:25-34; Matt 7:7-11; Matt 6:9-11; Ps 23

FOR SELF CONTROL
1 Ti 3:11; 2 Ti 3:3; Titus 2:2,12; 1 Pe 1:13, 1 Pe 1:6; 2 Tim 1:7; Pr 5:23,
16:32, 25:28.

FOR SPIRITUAL EYES
1 Cor 2:9-16; Eph 1:10-23; Rom 4:17

SPIRITUAL WARFARE
John 4:23; Gen 3:15; Ex 17:16; Eph 6:10-20; Isa 13:3; 2 Tim 1:7; 2 Cor 10:4; Rom 8:15; Eph 5:23

THE LORD IS MY SHEPHERD II
Ps 23

FOR THE ABILITY TO LOVE
Exodus 20:1-6; John 13:34; Matt 22:37; 1 Cor 13:1–8; John 3:16; Mark 12:30,31; Ezek 36:25,26; 1 John 4:8,16; Eph 3:19; Jer 31:3; 2 Cor 8:7

FOR THE BAPTISM OF THE HOLY SPIRIT
Eph 1:3-7; Col 2:9-10; Matt 3:11; John 7:37-38; Acts 1:8; John 20:22; Acts 2:4; Acts 11:16; Luke 24:49; John 15:26-27; John 16:13; Acts 5:12; Mark 16:17-18; John 10:28-30; Matt 6:9-13

FOR THE FRUITS OF THE SPIRIT
Gal 5:22,26; Deut 11:1; Josh 22:5; Matt 22:38; James 1:8; John 14:31; 1 John 4:7; Ps 4:7; Matt 2:10; Luke 6:21, 10:21; Rom 15:33; 2 Cor 13:11; 1 Thess 5:23; Heb13:20; 2 Cor 6:4-6; Eph 4:1-2; 1 Cor 1:1; 1 Cor 3:13

Ps 45:9; Luke 6:35; Matt 5:45; Rom 2:4; 1 Peter 2:3; Ps 25:8, 34:8, 86:5, 100:5, 118:1, 136:1, 145:9; Matt 19:17; 1 Peter 2:3; 1 Cor 15:34; Deut 7:9; 2 Peter 1:5-11; James 1:8; Matt 5:45, 6:4, 6,18; 1 Cor 10:13; 2 Cor 1:18-19; 2 Tim 2:13; Rev 3:14; 19:11; Col 1:4,7; 1 Tim 1:2; Ps 45:4; Is 53:7; Matt 21:41

THE LORD'S PRAYER
Matthew 6:9-15; 1 Cor 10:13; 2 Peter 2:9; James 1:12

FOR THE POWER TO PRAY
Rom 8:27-30; Heb 7:25; 1 John 2:1-6; Matt 26:64; Mark 14:62; Rom 8:38; 1 Peter 3:22; Rom 1:16; Mark 6:5, 11:22-26; James 5:16-18; Acts 8:1; Matt 28:18

FOR TRUSTING IN GOD
2 Sam 22:3; 2 Sam 22:31; 1 Ch 5:20; Ps 7:1, 16:1, 18:2, 18:30, 20:7, 25:2, 40:3, Ps 55:23, 56:4, 56:11, 73:28, 30:5; Mark 10:24; 2 Cor 1:9

FOR TRUTHFULNESS
Ex 34:6; Deut 32:4; Ps 25:10, 57:3, 89:14, 115:1, 96:13, 111:8; Isa 65:16; John 1:14; John 15:26; John 14:6; John 1:17; 1 Sam 15:29; Heb 6:18; James 1:17-18; John 14:17, 15:26, 16:13; Ps 71:22; John 8:32; John 8:31-32 Deut 32:4; Eph 6:11,14

FOR UNSELFISHNESS
1 John 4:8,117; John 15:9:15; John 3:16; Rom 5:5; Gal 5:1

WHEN I AM WEAK HE IS STRONG
2 Cor 12:5-10

WHEN I FALL DOWN
Prov 24:1-16

179

FOR BELIEVING GOD
Acts 27:22-26; 1 Cor 12:10; 1 John 4:1

FOR PRAYING GOD'S WORD
Ps 66:18-20; Isa 29:13; Jer 14:10-12; Ps 19:11; Mal 1:7-9; Matt 6:5-6; Luke 18:11-14; Heb 11:6; James 4:3; Isa 58:9-10; James 1:22; Mark 11:22-25, 11:25-26; John 14:13-14; John 15:7; Eph 6:8; 1 John 3:22; 1 John 5:14-15; 2 Chron 7:15; Rev 3:20-22

PUTTING ON THE WHOLE ARMOR OF GOD
Eph 6:10-18

Thoughts and Notes

Thoughts and Notes

Thoughts and Notes

www.ingramcontent.com/pod-product-compliance
Lightning Source LLC
Chambersburg PA
CBHW060531100426
42743CB00009B/1487